Diana Goodey Noel Goodey Miles Craven

GW01375475

Messages

Student's Book

3

CAMBRIDGE
UNIVERSITY PRESS

		Grammar and Expressions	Vocabulary and Pronunciation	Listening and Reading skills	Communicative tasks
Module 1 Present and past	Unit 1 Connections	• Questions and answers • Present continuous and present simple • *Expressions*: greetings and introductions	• Countries and nationalities • Language • Using numbers • *Pronunciation*: weak forms /ə/	• Listen to a song • Read a magazine article about the English language • Understand the main idea of an article • *Life and culture*: What a mixture!	• Ask questions when you meet new people • Talk about yourself and your friends • Describe someone you know • Write a report about your class
	Unit 2 Past events	• Past simple • Past continuous and past simple • *Expressions*: giving and accepting an apology	• Verbs describing actions • Adventure • Link words • *Pronunciation*: intonation in questions	• Listen to a story about a lucky discovery • Listen and complete a form • Read a short adventure story • Guess meaning from context • *Life and culture*: Journeys and explorers	• Write and act a conversation about events in the past • Interview a friend about a discovery • Write a short story
	Review	*Grammar check*	*Study skills*: Your coursebook	Progress check	*Coursework*: Home life
Module 2 Descriptions	Unit 3 People	• Comparatives and superlatives • *(not) as ... as* • *Expressions*: asking for a description	• Adjectives describing personality • The Internet • Opposites: *un-* + adjective • *Pronunciation*: stress in words	• Listen to a personality test • Read a Web page • Use pronouns and possessive adjectives • *Life and culture*: The British	• Write a description using comparatives and superlatives • Describe people's personality • Write a Web page about yourself
	Unit 4 Places	• Suggestions • Expressions of quantity: *too much/many, (not) enough, a lot of* • *Expressions*: responding to suggestions	• Places • School • Uses of *get* • *Pronunciation*: /k/ /p/ /t/	• Listen to someone talking about a place • Read an article about a Japanese student's day • Scan a text for information • *Life and culture*: Australia	• Plan a day out with friends • Describe a place you know, and things you like and don't like there • Write about a typical day
	Review	*Grammar check*	*Study skills*: Thinking about learning	Progress check	*Coursework*: Getting around
Module 3 The future	Unit 5 Goals	• Present continuous used for the future • The future with *going to* • The future with *will* and *going to* • *Expressions*: shopping	• Sports clothes • Competitive sport • Adjective/verb + preposition: *good at/worry about* • *Pronunciation*: /aɪ/ /ʊ/ /æ/	• Listen to a talk about a cycling trip • Read an interview with a young athlete • Skim a text for the general idea • *Life and culture*: The history of the Olympics	• Talk about future plans • Talk about the future and make offers • Make a conversation in a shop • Interview a friend and then write about him/her
	Unit 6 Choices	• First conditional • The future with *will* and *might* • *will/won't + probably* • *Expressions*: polite requests	• At the table • Artificial intelligence • Compound nouns: *coffee maker* • *Pronunciation*: /e/ /eɪ/ /ʌ/	• Listen to a song • Read an article about artificial intelligence • Identify the topic • *Life and culture*: Journey into space	• Make a conversation in a restaurant • Describe things that aren't certain and things that are probable in the future • Write about future plans • Make predictions about life in the future
	Review	*Grammar check*	*Study skills*: Making a vocabulary notebook	Progress check	*Coursework*: Shopping in London

Module 1

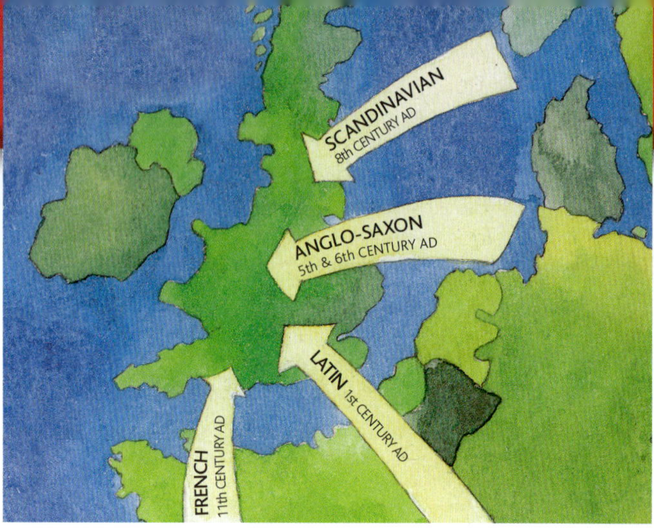

Present and past

In Module 1 Steps 1 and 2 you study

Grammar

- Questions and answers
- Present continuous and present simple
- Past simple
- Past continuous and past simple

Vocabulary

- Countries and nationalities
- Verbs describing actions

Expressions

- Greetings and introductions
- Giving and accepting an apology

so that you can

- Ask questions when you meet new people
- Greet and introduce people in different ways
- Describe nationality and say where people come from
- Talk about yourself and your friends
- Talk about events in the past
- Say that you're sorry
- Describe events in the past that are interrupted by other events

Life and culture

What a mixture!
Journeys and explorers

Coursework 1

Part 1 Home life
You write about home life in your country.

If you stay with an English family, what will life be like? I don't know if the Grants are a typical English family, but I'll tell you about my life at their flat in north-west London.

During the week, the day starts at about 7.15. We have our breakfast in the kitchen. Tim and Penny Grant always have toast and coffee, but a lot of English people prefer tea. Charlie (Tim and Penny's son) has orange juice and cereal. If everyone is in a hurry, we don't have time to sit down. I often make a sandwich to take to the language school with me.

Tim and Penny leave the flat at about eight o'clock. They go to work on the tube. I get the bus to school. I usually walk to the bus stop with Charlie. A lot of British people travel to work by car. The roads are often very busy, especially during the 'rush hour' – the time when people go to work in the morning and go home at the end of the day.

At the weekend, Charlie and Tim sometimes go to a football match, and Tim always washes the car. Penny does the housework and Tim does the shopping at the supermarket near the flat. It's open nearly all the time and it's huge, with a big car park. Sometimes we go to the cinema, or we go for a walk on Hampstead Heath. Sometimes

In Step 3 you ...

read

- A magazine article about the English language
- A short adventure story

study

- Numbers
- Link words
- Understanding the main idea
- Guessing meaning from context

so that you can

- Write a report about your class
- Write a short story

What's it about?

What can you say about the pictures?

Now match the pictures with sentences 1–4.

1 The Grants always have coffee and toast for breakfast.
2 He made a spear to catch the fish in the lake.
3 Why is Ana crying?
4 Amelia Earhart was flying to Australia when her plane crashed.

a

b

c

d

Coursework

My guidebook

In Book 3 you study

- a guidebook for visitors to an English-speaking country

so that you can

- make a guidebook for an English-speaking visitor to your country

Your Coursework has got six parts:

Part 1 Home life
You write about home life in your country.

Part 2 Getting around
You write about interesting places in your country.

Part 3 Shopping in London
You write about shopping in your town or in your capital city.

Part 4 Useful information
You write some useful information for a visitor to your country.

Part 5 Mini phrase book
You write a mini phrase book for a visitor to your country.

Part 6 Entertainment
You write about entertainment in your country.

1 Connections

STEP 1

In Step 1 you study
- questions and answers
- greetings and introductions

so that you can
- ask questions when you meet new people
- greet people
- introduce people

1 Share your ideas

What can you say about the photo? Where are the boy and girl? What do you think they're saying?

They're in a park.

2 Reading and speaking

Where do you come from?

a Which questions do you think the boy is asking? Choose eight questions from the list.

1. What's your name?
2. Why are you laughing?
3. Where do you come from?
4. Have you got any friends here?
5. Do you live in Mexico City?
6. Are you all right?
7. What do you think of London?
8. What are you doing in England?
9. Do you play tennis?
10. What's the matter?

b Complete the conversation with questions from 2a.

JAY: [a] *Are you all right?*
ANA: No, I'm not.
JAY: [b] ....
ANA: I'm homesick.
JAY: [c] ....
ANA: I come from Mexico.
JAY: [d] ....
ANA: No, I don't. I live in Veracruz.
JAY: [e] ....
ANA: I'm studying English. I'm staying with a family here.
JAY: [f] ....
ANA: I like it, but I sometimes feel a bit homesick.
JAY: [g] ....
ANA: No, I haven't.
JAY: [h] ....
ANA: Ana.
JAY: Pleased to meet you, Ana. I'm Jay, Jay Sayer. Er ... do you fancy an ice cream?

Listen and check.

c If you have time, practise the conversation between Jay and Ana.

Revision

3 Grammar revision *Questions and answers*

Complete the questions with *is/are, do/does, has/have*.

Is Ana Mexican? – Yes, she **is**.
.... she happy? – No, she **isn't**.
.... Jay and Ana in the park? – Yes, they **are**.
.... they both speak English? – Yes, they **do**.
Does Ana come from London? – No, she **doesn't**.
.... she like London? – Yes, she **does**.
.... she got any English friends? – No, she **hasn't**.
.... Ana and Jay got an ice cream? – No, they **haven't**.
Where .... Ana live? – In Veracruz.
Why .... she crying? – Because she's homesick.

G ▸ 1a, 2a

4 Practice

a Put the words in the right order and make questions.

1 Are Jay and Ana old friends?

1 old / Ana / are / friends / Jay / and ?
2 they / where / are ?
3 Mexican / Jay / is ?
4 English / got / friends / Ana / any / has ?
5 she / homesick / is ?
6 from / she / where / come / does ?
7 studying / what's / Ana ?
8 Veracruz / live / Jay / does / in ?

b Now ask and answer the questions in 4a.

> Are Jay and Ana old friends?
>
> No, they aren't.

5 Key expressions *Greetings and introductions*

a Read and complete the dialogues.

1
This .... Mrs Jones, the head teacher.
How do you do, Mrs Jones?
How do you do?
2
Hi, Jenny. How .... you today?
I .... fine, thanks.
3
This is my friend Tom.
Nice to .... you, Tom.

Listen and check.

b Match the expressions with the explanations. How do you say these expressions in your language?

1 Hi!/Hello! How are you?
2 Nice to meet you. / Pleased to meet you.
3 How do you do?

a This is a formal greeting. You can use it when you meet an adult for the first time.
b You often say this when you see a friend.
c You say this when you meet someone for the first time. It's friendly but it can be formal or informal.

Remember!

How do you do? *isn't really a question, and the response is* How do you do?

6 Key pronunciation
Weak forms /ə/

Listen and repeat the sentences.

1 How are /ə/ you today?
2 Where are /ə/ you from?
3 How do you /djə/ do?
4 Where do you /djə/ live?

7 Writing and speaking
Meeting people

Use what you know

Imagine you're meeting an English teenager for the first time. Work with a friend and make a short conversation.

A: Hi! I'm David. What's your name?
B: My name's Max. Nice to meet you, David.
A: Where do you come from, Max?

Practise your conversation.

STEP 2

In Step 2 you study
- countries and nationalities
- present continuous and present simple

so that you can
- say where people come from and their nationality
- talk about yourself and your friends

1 Key vocabulary *Countries and nationalities*

a Match the countries with the nationalities.

Country Poland *Nationality Polish*

Polish Australian Italy French Argentina British Greek American
Britain Canadian Mexico Spain Japanese the USA France Argentinian
Poland Australia Spanish Greece Mexican Japan Canada Italian

Listen and check.

b Can you add any more countries and nationalities to your list? You've got two minutes!

c **What about you?** Say your country/town and nationality, or talk about your favourite star.

My favourite star is Johnny Depp. I think he's American.

Remember!

We use a capital letter for the names of countries, nationalities and languages.
I live in **J**apan. I'm **J**apanese. I speak **J**apanese and **E**nglish.

2 Presentation *What are they doing?*

a Think of at least two questions about the photo, then ask a friend your questions.

b Close your book and listen to the text about Ana. What's she thinking about?

When she's at home in Veracruz, Ana usually starts the day with some *chilaquiles* and a hot chocolate. She always has breakfast with her sister Clara, and they talk about their plans for the day.

Now, of course, everything's different. At the moment she's sitting in the kitchen with her English family, the Grants. She's having a cup of coffee and a piece of toast. The Grants always have coffee and toast for breakfast. It's raining outside and the Grants are talking about the weather again. But Ana isn't listening. She's looking at the rain and she's thinking about her sister, at home in Veracruz.

c Listen again and follow in your book. Ask and answer the questions.

1 What does Ana usually have for breakfast?
2 What's she having today?
3 Is she talking to her sister?
4 Does her sister live in Veracruz?
5 What are the Grants doing?
6 What's Ana doing?

3 Key grammar *Present continuous and present simple*

a Look at the examples and complete the explanations.

At the moment, Ana's sitting in the kitchen.
We use the present .... to talk about actions in progress at the moment.

The Grants always have coffee and toast.
We use the present .... to talk about habits, or things that are generally true.

G 1, 2

b Look at the text again and find at least two more examples of the present continuous and the present simple.

4 Practice

a Complete the sentences with the present continuous or the present simple.

1 The Grants often *talk* (*talk*) about the weather.
2 Ana .... (*not talk*) to her sister at the moment.
3 Ana .... (*not like*) tea.
4 At home in Mexico, she usually .... (*have*) hot chocolate for breakfast.
5 The Grants .... (*live*) in London.
6 The weather isn't good today. It .... (*rain*).
7 It's 7.30 am in London and Ana .... (*get up*). But in Veracruz it's 1.30 am and Clara .... (*go*) home after a party.
8 Clara .... (*send*) her sister a text message nearly every day.

b **What about you?** How many true sentences can you write about yourself, using the present continuous and the present simple? You've got two minutes!

At the moment, I'm writing a sentence in English.
I like music and swimming.

Try this!
How many days of the week can you write using these letters? You can use each letter more than once.
W T U N A H E O Y D M C N R F S

5 Listening and speaking *Song*

a Listen to the song. How many times do you hear the word *jeans*?

b Listen again. How many of these things are mentioned?

6 Speaking *Who is it?*

Use what you know

Describe someone in the class. Use the present continuous and the present simple.

He's wearing a black sweater.
He plays a lot of volleyball.

Can your friend guess who it is?

Is it Hugo?

No, it isn't.

STEP 3

In Step 3 you
- read a magazine article about the English language
- practise using numbers

so that you can
- write a report about your class

1 Share your ideas *Learning English*

Why is English a useful language? Think of at least three reasons.

It's an international language.

2 Reading

a Read the text. How many of your reasons can you find?

ENGLISH WORLDWIDE!

One World Magazine

This month we look at how the English language brings people together.

Did you know that a quarter of all the people on Earth speak English? That's 1.5 billion people!

This is **Tara**. She's from New Zealand and English is her first language. About 450 million people speak English as a first language in countries like Britain, the USA, Australia and New Zealand.

Sandro is from Puerto Rico but now he lives in New York. His first language is Spanish, but he speaks English too. Thirty-six million people in the USA come from Latin America. They learn English as a second language because they live in an English-speaking country. About 375 million people across

the world use English as a second language. In India, for example, there are over 350 different languages, so people often use English to communicate with each other.

Mohammed is Egyptian. He's learning English at school. About 750 million people learn English as a foreign language. They use it in their job, when they travel abroad, or when they want to understand English films or songs.

English is the main language in international business, in science and technology, in sport and pop music. For example, nearly 70% of the world's scientists read scientific texts in English. On the Internet, over 60% of home pages and about 85% of emails are in English.

Language is a key to the outside world. It helps you to connect with other people. At the moment, about a billion people are learning English, so you aren't alone!

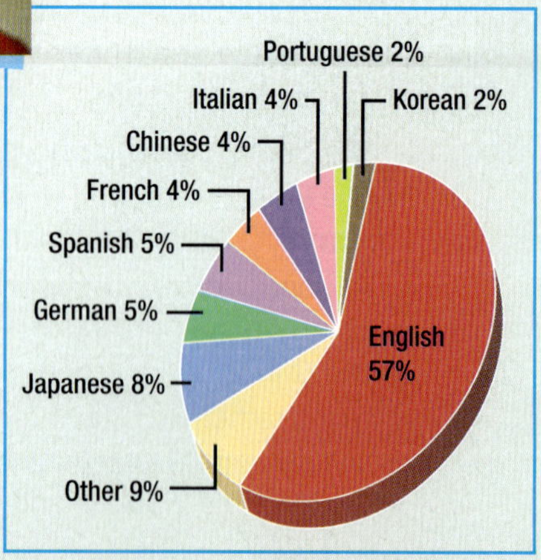

The languages of Internet users

b **Comprehension check**

Listen, and read the text again. Then match 1–7 with a–g and make sentences.

1 English is the first language of
2 There are three hundred and seventy-five million
3 There are three hundred and fifty
4 For thirty-six million Americans
5 Three quarters of a billion people
6 Seventy per cent of the world's scientists
7 About eighty-five per cent of emails

a different languages in India.
b learn English as a foreign language.
c four hundred and fifty million people.
d are in English.
e Spanish is their first language.
f speakers of English as a second language.
g can read texts in English.

c **Reading skills** *Understanding the main idea*

1 What is the topic of the text?
a culture b language c countries

2 What do you think is the main idea of the text? Read the beginning and the end again, then choose the best answer.

It's about ...

a all the different languages in the world.
b English as an international language.
c English people all over the world.

3 Word work *Numbers*

a Match the words on the left with the figures on the right.

1	a thousand	a	2.75
2	six thousand	b	1,000
3	a million	c	$4\frac{1}{4}$
4	one and a half	d	75%
5	two point seven five	e	6,000
6	seventy-five per cent	f	$1\frac{3}{4}$
7	one and three quarters	g	1,000,000
8	four and a quarter	h	$1\frac{1}{2}$

b Write the underlined words in figures.

1 8,000

1 Eight thousand people.
2 Three quarters of the class.
3 Five and a half years.
4 Nine point two litres of water.
5 A quarter of the population.
6 Sixty per cent of television programmes.
7 A million dollars.
8 Eighteen per cent of the world's scientists.

c **Test a friend** Write a number in words. Can your friend write it in figures?

A: Three million, two hundred and sixty-eight thousand, nine hundred and one.
B: 3,268,901

Remember!

We use a hyphen in: seventy-five ninety-two

Writing guide *Writing a report*

- Think of a title and write the date.
  Statistics about our class 5th October
- Introduce your report.
  We asked questions about using English. These are our results.
- Start each new fact on a new line.
  Two people in the class have got an English-speaking friend.
  Three quarters of the class watch films in English.

4 Speaking and writing *About my class*

Use what you know

Ask your friends about using English, for example:

Do you think English is useful?
When do you use English?
Have you got any English-speaking friends?
Do you watch films in English?

With your teacher, choose three or four questions to ask the whole class. Put the answers on the board, then write a report. Follow the Writing guide.

Extra exercises

1 Choose the right answers.

1 Are you and Susan hungry?
  a No, we aren't.
  b No, we don't.
  c No, we haven't.

2 Do Jane and Tom go abroad a lot?
  a Yes, they are.
  b Yes, they do.
  c Yes, they have.

3 Does Kevin use a computer for his homework?
  a Yes, he has.
  b Yes, he is.
  c Yes, he does.

4 Is English your first language?
  a No, I haven't.
  b No, it isn't.
  c No, I'm not.

5 Has Tina got any English friends?
  a Yes, she is.
  b Yes, she does.
  c Yes, she has.

2 Choose the right words and make complete sentences.

1 Sue usually (*gets / is getting*) up at seven o'clock.
2 James (*doesn't write / isn't writing*) an email at the moment.
3 Over 1.5 billion people (*speak / are speaking*) English.
4 (*Do you stay / Are you staying*) in a hotel or with friends this week?
5 Oh no! It (*rains / 's raining*). Where's my umbrella?
6 Sometimes I (*feel / 'm feeling*) homesick.

3 Make questions for these answers.

1 Where are you going?

1 I'm going to the cinema.
2 In London.
3 Yes, a bit. We learnt it at school.
4 No, he lives in a flat.
5 About 1.5 billion, I think.
6 Because it's funny.
7 I can't find my mobile.
8 No, she isn't. She's homesick.

4 Complete the conversation.

A: 1 *What are you doing?*
B: I'm using the Internet.
A: 2 ....
B: No, I'm not studying. I'm playing a game called *Wizard Wars*.
A: 3 ....
B: I'm playing with my friend Gavin.
A: 4 ....
B: He lives in Manchester.
A: 5 ....
B: Yes, we play this game every day.
A: 6 ....
B: I'm winning!

5 Match 1–8 with a–h. Then write four short conversations.

1e This is Mr Wilson, the science teacher.
6b How do you do, Mr Wilson?

1 This is Mr Wilson,	a you all right?
2 Hi, Steve. How	b do, Mr Wilson?
3 This is my	c a cold.
4 Are	d you, Ben.
5 I'm	e the science teacher.
6 How do you	f fine, thanks.
7 No, I've got	g best friend, Ben.
8 Nice to meet	h are you?

6 Put the letters in the right order and find ten nationalities. Then write the country for each nationality.

1 Mexican - Mexico

1 ECIXMNA 2 AILANTI 3 IADNCANA
4 NEARIGTNIAN 5 SIPSNAH 6 TRHIISB
7 KEGER 8 CAMIAREN 9 NRFHCE
10 NEPSAJAE

7 How do you say these sentences in your language?

1 Pleased to meet you.
2 How do you do?
3 Do you fancy an ice cream?
4 What's the matter?
5 Mike's an old friend.
6 This is our teacher, Mrs Webster.

Extra reading

Life and culture

What a mixture!

Are there any English words in your language? How many do you know?

The English language is a mixture of several different languages – mainly Latin, Anglo-Saxon, Scandinavian and French. The word *dentist*, for example, comes from the Latin 'dentes', meaning *teeth*. This explains why there are often two or three words with the same meaning, for example, *to begin, to start, to commence*. It is also the reason why English spelling can be so strange. We 'write' (/raɪt/) a question and we give the 'right' (/raɪt/) answer – the pronunciation is the same but the spelling is different. Today, the British use the Roman alphabet (*a, b, c*), Arabic numerals (*1, 2, 3*), the names of Viking gods for days of the week, and even old French – for example, when the Queen writes 'Le Roi le veult' to show her agreement to a new law in parliament. But how did all this happen?

The first inhabitants of the British Isles were hunters. About five thousand years ago, settlers from Europe started to arrive. Celts, Romans, Angles and Saxons, and then Vikings all invaded at different times. For 200 years, England had Anglo-Saxon kings and Danish kings. In 1066, the French arrived on the south coast of England. William, Duke of Normandy, defeated the Saxon King Harold at the Battle of Hastings and became the king of England. For the next 300 years, the kings of England spoke French and they ruled a large part of France too.

In the fifteenth century, England lost her lands in France, and the French language began to lose its importance. At the same time, the first English books appeared. After that, English finally became the official written and spoken language of the country.

ABOUT THE ENGLISH LANGUAGE

There are nearly 800,000 words in the English language. But don't worry! You only need about 5,000 words if you want to have an everyday conversation in English.

Task

Read the text and these sentences. For each sentence write T (true), F (false) or ? (the text doesn't say). Correct the false sentences.

1 English contains words from a lot of different languages.
2 English spelling is very simple.
3 The word 'Thursday' comes from the name of a Viking god.
4 The Queen speaks French when she is at the Houses of Parliament.
5 *Write* and *right* have got the same sound.
6 The French won the Battle of Hastings.
7 The king of England sometimes lived in France.
8 English became the official language about five hundred years ago.

2 Past events

STEP 1

In Step 1 you study	so that you can
• past simple	• talk about events in the past
• giving and accepting an apology	• say that you're sorry

1 Share your ideas

What can you say about pictures 1–8? Use the past simple. What did Jay and Ana do?

> Picture 1 – Jay had a shower. He got ready.
> Picture 6 – He got off the bus outside the cinema.

1
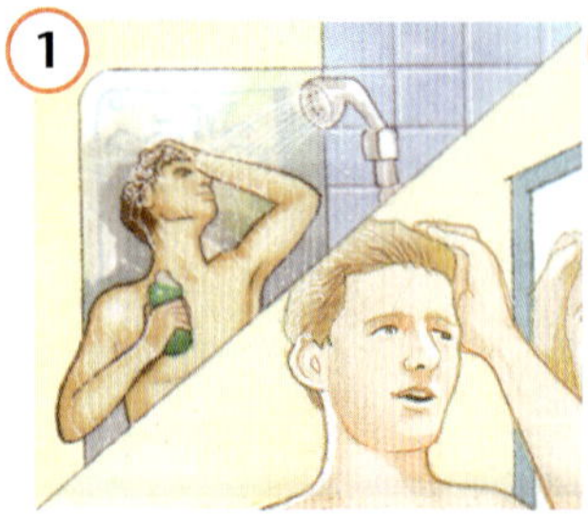

2

3

4

5

6

7

8

2 Presentation *Did you forget?*

a Close your book and listen. Is Jay angry?

Ana is at the Grants' flat. The phone's ringing.

ANA: Hello.
JAY: Hello, Ana. It's Jay here. I'm outside the cinema. Er ... did you forget?
ANA: No, of course I didn't. I went to the cinema, but you weren't there.
JAY: But I got here at twenty past seven.
ANA: Well, I left the flat at seven and got the tube. Then I waited for you outside the cinema.
JAY: That's funny. I didn't see you.
ANA: And I didn't see you. I waited until eight o'clock, then I came home again.
JAY: Hang on a minute! Did you go to the Odeon?
ANA: The Odeon? No, I think it was the Empire.
JAY: Oh, no! You went to the wrong cinema.
ANA: Oh! I'm sorry, Jay.
JAY: That's OK. Don't worry about it. It's my fault. I didn't explain clearly.
ANA: That's all right. It doesn't matter.
JAY: Er ... are you free tomorrow night?

b Listen again and follow in your book. Then answer the questions.

1 What time did Ana leave her flat?
2 How did she get to the cinema?
3 Where did she wait?
4 Did she see Jay?
5 What did she do after that?

c Look at the pictures and ask and answer the same questions about Jay.

> 1 What time did Jay leave his flat?

3 Key grammar *Past simple*

Complete the examples.

Affirmative	Negative
Jay **was** there at 7.30.	Ana .... there.
Jay **waited** outside the Odeon.	He .... **wait** outside the Empire.
Ana .... to the Empire.	She **didn't go** to the Odeon.

Questions and short answers

Did Jay **see** Ana? – No, he ....
.... Ana **go** home? – Yes, she **did**.

G 3

4 Practice

a **Put the verbs in the past simple. Then put the sentences in the right order and make a story.**

1g Yesterday afternoon, Ana's English lesson finished at half past three.

- a Ana .... (*look*) around and .... (*see*) a record shop on the other side of the road.
- b She .... (*catch*) the bus outside the school and .... (*sit*) by the window.
- c She .... (*not see*) any paintings but she .... (*have*) a really nice afternoon!
- d So she .... (*go*) into the record shop.
- e Ten minutes later she .... (*get off*) the bus, but she .... (*not get off*) at Trafalgar Square.
- f She .... (*listen*) to her favourite group, and .... (*buy*) a CD for her sister Clara.
- g Yesterday afternoon, Ana's English lesson .... (*finish*) at half past three.
- h She .... (*be*) in Piccadilly Circus.
- i She .... (*decide*) to go to the National Gallery in Trafalgar Square because she .... (*want*) to see the paintings there.

b **Test a friend** **Write at least two questions about the story. Ask and answer the questions.**

Where did Ana get off the bus?

5 Key pronunciation
Intonation in questions

Listen and repeat the questions.

1. Where did you go? ↘
2. Did you go to the cinema? ↗
3. What did you see? ↘
4. Was it good? ↗

Try this!

Match the two halves of each word and find eight verbs in the past simple.

LOO NT TED PEARED WE ME KED
WAI GHT CA ARRIV CAU HT DISAP
BOUG ED

6 Key expressions *Apologies*

a **Put the sentences in the right order and make two conversations.**

1

2

1 – Yes, you are.
– That's all right. Don't worry about it.
– Oh! I'm sorry.
– Am I in your seat?

2 – I'm sorry. It isn't my fault. The bus was late.
– Come on, then. Let's get our tickets.
– At last! It's quarter past eight. Why are you so late?
– Oh, I see. Well, it doesn't matter. We've got five minutes.

b **Listen and check, then practise the conversations.**

7 Writing and speaking *The wrong place!*

Use what you know

Look again at the conversation between Jay and Ana. Work in pairs and write a similar telephone conversation.

Where are you now? What time did you get there? What did you do? Did you go to the right place? Where did your friend go?

Practise your conversation.

STEP 2

In Step 2 you study
- verbs describing actions
- past continuous and past simple

so that you can
- describe events in the past

1 Key vocabulary *Verbs describing actions*

Match the verbs with the pictures. You've got two minutes!

fall sail hit land
jump fly crash sink

Listen and check.

2 Presentation *What were they doing?*

a Make five sentences from the jigsaw then match them with the pictures.

1d The Titanic was a famous ship. It was sailing to New York when it hit an iceberg and sank. Picture C

Listen and check.

b Ask and answer the questions.

1. Where was the *Titanic* going?
2. Why did it sink?
3. Was Newton eating an apple?
4. Did he fall and hurt his head?
5. When did Amelia Earhart disappear?
6. Did Columbus want to go to the Bahamas?
7. What was Archimedes doing when he got his new idea?

1. The *Titanic* was a famous ship. It was sailing to New York
2. Isaac Newton was a scientist. He was sitting under a tree
3. Amelia Earhart was one of the first women pilots. She was flying to Australia
4. Columbus was an explorer. He was trying to find India
5. Archimedes was a Greek inventor. He was having a bath

3 Key grammar *Past continuous and past simple*

Look at the examples and complete the explanations.

In 1665, Isaac Newton **made** an important discovery.
We use the past .... for completed actions in the past.

He **was studying** physics at Cambridge University.
We use the past .... to describe the situation at a particular time in the past.

He **was sitting** under a tree when an apple **fell** on his head.
We use the .... and the .... together when one action was in progress and another action interrupted it.

fell
←——————↓——————→
was sitting

G→ 4

4 Practice

a Complete the sentences with the past continuous and the past simple.

1 When Jay ....*arrived*.......... (*arrive*) at school this morning, his friends ..*were playing*.. (*play*) cards.
2 Clara .... (*have*) a bath when the telephone .... (*ring*). It .... (*be*) her sister Ana.
3 I .... (*wait*) for the bus when I .... (*see*) Tom. He .... (*wear*) his new jeans.
4 Jay .... (*meet*) Ana when they .... (*sit*) in Hyde Park. She .... (*cry*) and he .... (*start*) to talk to her.

b **What about you?** Ask and answer.

What was happening when you arrived at school this morning?

Paulo was talking to Leo and Maria was doing her homework.

when

a her plane crashed and she disappeared.
b an apple fell on his head.
c he jumped up and shouted 'Eureka!'
d it hit an iceberg and sank.
e he landed in the Bahamas.

C

D

E

5 Listening *A lucky discovery*

a Listen to the conversation between Mark Taylor and a reporter. Answer these questions.

1 Where was Mark when he made his discovery?
2 What was he doing?

b Listen again, then complete the sentences.

1 Mark found some Roman coins in ....
2 He showed them to ....
3 They went to ....
4 The police telephoned ....
5 The museum gave Mark ....
6 Mark bought a new ....

c Copy and complete the form.

Swaffam Museum Payment form

Name: ....
Item(s) found: ....
Location: ....
Price: ....

6 Writing and speaking *Discoveries*

Use what you know

Imagine you recently made an interesting discovery. Write answers to these questions.

Where were you? What were you doing?
What did you find? What did you do?
How much money did you get?
What did you do with the money?

Now interview a friend about his/her discovery.

STEP 3

In Step 3 you
- read a short adventure story
- study link words

so that you can
- write a short story

1 Share your ideas *Stories*

What kind of stories do you like?

adventure stories crime stories
fantasy science fiction
ghost stories love stories

I read a lot of science fiction.

2 Reading

a **Read the text quickly. Has the story got a happy ending?**

Survival!

Teenager Brian Robeson was travelling from the USA to Canada to see his father. He was the only passenger in a small plane, high above the Canadian mountains, when suddenly the pilot had a heart attack and died!

Brian was terrified. He was shaking, but he tried not to panic. Below him, he could see a lake. He turned the plane towards the lake and, incredibly, he landed on the water. Brian got out of the plane just before it sank. He swam to the beach and then he fell asleep, exhausted.

When Brian woke up the next morning, he was cold and hungry. The quiet boy from New York only had the clothes he was wearing and a small hatchet (a present from his mother). Then he remembered a TV programme about how to survive in the wild. He made a shelter with grass and some branches from the trees. He used his hatchet to cut wood and start a fire. He ate fruit from the forest. He made a spear to catch fish in the lake, and he made a bow and arrow to kill rabbits and birds.

One night there was a fierce storm and the plane came to the surface of the lake. Brian swam to the plane and found some food, a knife and a small radio. He tried to call for help on the radio, but he wasn't sure how it worked.

One day, a few weeks later, Brian was fishing by the lake when he heard a noise. He could see a plane above the trees. It was looking for him! Quickly, he made a fire, and the pilot saw the smoke. After fifty-four days in the Canadian woods, Brian's amazing adventure was finally over.

7

b Reading skills *Guessing meaning from context*

1 Find these words in the text. Read what comes before and after. What do you think the words mean?

heart attack   shaking   exhausted
branches   surface

2 Now find these words. Can you guess what they mean? Can you see these items in the picture?

hatchet   shelter   spear   bow   arrow

c Comprehension check

Listen, and read the text again. Then answer the questions.

1 Where was Brian going when his adventure began?
2 Where did he land?
3 Could Brian swim?
4 How did he know how to survive?
5 Where did he sleep?
6 What did he eat?
7 Why did his plane reappear?
8 What did Brian find on the plane?
9 Did he know how to use the radio?
10 What was Brian doing when help arrived?

Remember!

The past tense of can *is* could.
He **could** see a lake. Brian **could** swim well.

3 Word work *Link words*

a Look at the words in the box. Do you know what they all mean?

after	and	before	but	suddenly
then	when			

b Choose the best link word, a, b or c, to complete each sentence.

1 Brian was flying to the USA .... the pilot had a heart attack.
a and   b when   c then

2 .... the pilot died, Brian flew the plane.
a Then   b After   c Suddenly

3 He was terrified, ... he didn't panic.
a but   b then   c and

4 He landed on the water .... swam to the beach.
a when   b and   c before

5 .... he got to the beach, he fell asleep.
a When   b Before   c But

6 He made a fire and .... he cooked some food.
a when   b before   c then

7 He was fishing and .... he heard a noise.
a before   b when   c suddenly

8 He quickly lit a fire .... the plane disappeared.
a then   b before   c suddenly

Writing guide *Writing a story*

- **Paragraph 1**

Set the scene. Say when and where the event took place, who you were with and what you were doing.

One day last summer I was ...
I was with my ...   We were ...-ing

- **Paragraph 2**

Develop the story. Say what happened next.

Suddenly ...   I/We ...

- **Paragraph 3**

Finish the story.

Then we ...

4 Writing *A short story*

Use what you know

Imagine you were going somewhere when you had a problem. Write a short story.

When was it? Where were you?
Who were you with? What were you doing?
What happened next? What did you do?
Then what happened?

Read your story to a friend.

Extra exercises

1 Complete the conversations. Use *one* word.

1 A: Ouch! You're standing on my foot.
  B: Oh, I'm .... I didn't see you.

2 A: We haven't got any coffee.
  B: That's all .... I'll have tea.

3 A: Sorry I'm late. The traffic was terrible.
  B: That's OK. It doesn't .... You're here now.

4 A: Oh no! There's water all over the kitchen floor.
  B: Well, don't shout at me. It isn't my ....

5 A: Oh dear. Is your soup a bit cold?
  B: Don't .... about it. It's fine.

2 Read the text and choose the right words for each space.

Carol and Fiona [1].......... to go to Paris on holiday, because Carol had some friends there. They [2].......... much money so they [3].......... to go by coach. After eleven hours on the coach they [4].......... in Paris, exhausted. When they [5].......... the coach, Carol's friends [6].......... for them. It was the beginning of an amazing holiday.

1	a wanted	b were wanting	c did want
2	a weren't having	b didn't have	c had not
3	a decided	b were deciding	c were decided
4	a were arriving	b arrived	c arrive
5	a get off	b were getting off	c got off
6	a waited	b were waiting	c waiting

3 Complete the conversations.

1b

1 What was John doing when you saw him?
  a He did his homework.
  b He was playing football.
  c He's talking to Jane.

2 I went to the cinema yesterday.
  a Who were you going with?
  b What film did you see?
  c Why don't you ask me?

3 Why didn't you answer the phone when I rang?
  a I had a bath.
  b I'm not at home.
  c I was having dinner.

4 I saw Susan last night at a party.
  a Was she dancing with you?
  b Did you dance with her?
  c Where was she?

5 Did your parents give you that phone?
  a No, I bought it.
  b They bought it.
  c Yes, they were buying it.

4 Choose the right words.

1 Dan was driving home when his car .... a tree.
  a hit b crashed c fell

2 There was a fierce storm and a lot of boats .... because of the bad weather.
  a sailed b landed c sank

3 When the President went into the room everyone .... up and smiled.
  a jumped b flew c fell

4 The plane .... in Madrid and everyone got off.
  a flew b landed c crashed

5 Martin .... and hurt his knee when he was playing football yesterday.
  a hit b fell c crashed

5 Complete the sentences. Use the past continuous or the past simple.

1 It .... when I .... this morning. (*rain, get up*)
2 Angela .... me yesterday evening. We .... dinner when she .... (*phone, have, call*)
3 Steve's grandfather .... a heart attack when he .... to Australia. (*have, fly*)
4 I .... outside the cinema when I .... an accident. (*wait, see*)
5 An old woman .... across the road when a taxi .... her. (*walk, hit*)
6 Penny .... Tim when she .... through Hyde Park. (*meet, run*)

6 How do you say these sentences in your language?

1 Hang on a minute.
2 That's funny. I didn't see you at the party.
3 Are you free on Saturday night?
4 It isn't my fault.
5 Don't worry about it.
6 It doesn't matter.

Extra reading

Life and culture

Journeys and explorers

Do you know the names of any explorers? Why are they famous?

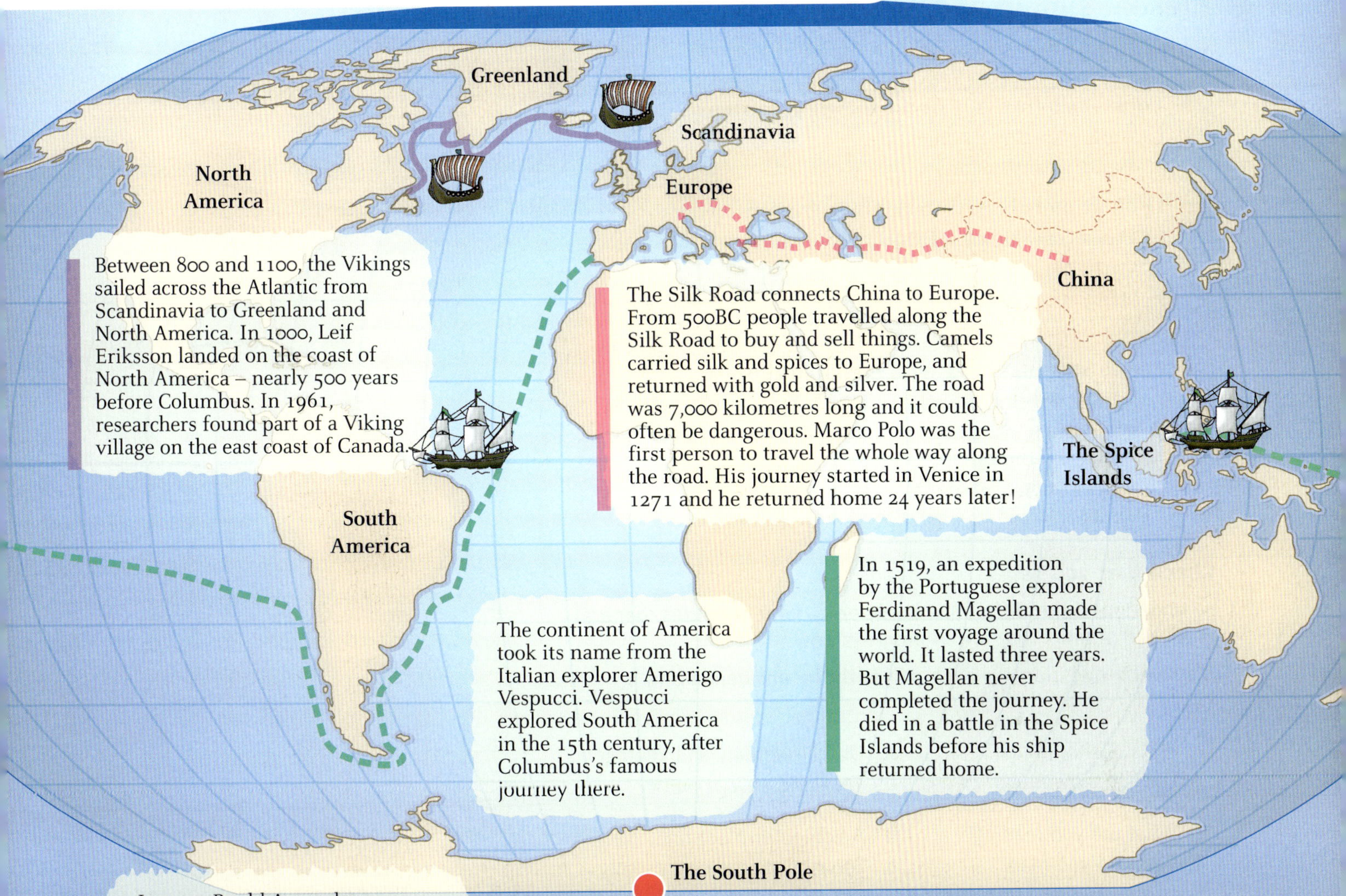

Between 800 and 1100, the Vikings sailed across the Atlantic from Scandinavia to Greenland and North America. In 1000, Leif Eriksson landed on the coast of North America – nearly 500 years before Columbus. In 1961, researchers found part of a Viking village on the east coast of Canada.

The Silk Road connects China to Europe. From 500BC people travelled along the Silk Road to buy and sell things. Camels carried silk and spices to Europe, and returned with gold and silver. The road was 7,000 kilometres long and it could often be dangerous. Marco Polo was the first person to travel the whole way along the road. His journey started in Venice in 1271 and he returned home 24 years later!

The continent of America took its name from the Italian explorer Amerigo Vespucci. Vespucci explored South America in the 15th century, after Columbus's famous journey there.

In 1519, an expedition by the Portuguese explorer Ferdinand Magellan made the first voyage around the world. It lasted three years. But Magellan never completed the journey. He died in a battle in the Spice Islands before his ship returned home.

In 1911 Roald Amundsen from Norway became the first person to reach the South Pole. A British team of explorers, with their leader Robert Scott, were trying to get there at the same time. The Norwegian team arrived at the Pole on 14th December, 33 days before Scott's team. Scott and his four men all died on their return journey.

ABOUT EXPLORERS

The early explorers didn't have maps or compasses. They used the stars to help them navigate.

Task

Look at the map and the information, then answer the questions.

1. Where did the Silk Road start and finish?
2. How did people carry things along the Silk Road?
3. When did Marco Polo return home to Venice?
4. Who were the first people to land in North America?
5. Where did Leif Eriksson come from?
6. Where does the name 'America' come from?
7. Where did Magellan's expedition go?
8. When did Roald Amundsen reach the South Pole?
9. When did the British team get there?
10. Which explorers in the texts didn't return home?

Module 1 Review

Grammar check

1 Present simple and present continuous

Work it out for yourself

A Look at picture A. Choose the right sentence.

1 Mario's speaking Italian.
2 Mario speaks Italian.

B Look at picture B. Choose the right sentences.

1 Mario's speaking English.
2 Mario doesn't speak Italian.
3 Mario speaks Italian and English.
4 Mario isn't speaking Italian.

C Match sentences 1–3 with explanations a–c.

1 Mario's visiting England.
2 Mario often visits his cousin in London.
3 A lot of Italians visit London.

a a habit, a regular activity
b a fact that is generally true
c an action that is in progress now

Check that you can

1.1 • **understand the difference between regular activities/general facts and actions that are in progress now.**

Match the questions in each pair with the answers a and b.

1b

1 Is it snowing much?	a Only in January and February.
2 Does it snow much?	b Yes. Let's stay at home.
3 What are you reading?	a A computer magazine.
4 What do you read?	b Teenage magazines, usually.
5 What are you doing?	a I write books for children.
6 What do you do?	b I'm writing an email.
7 Is he speaking Chinese?	a Yes, he goes to China every year.
8 Does he speak Chinese?	b Yes, he is.
9 Are you walking to school?	a No, I'm going to the dentist.
10 Do you walk to school?	b No, I don't. I get the bus.

1.2 • **use the present continuous and the present simple.**

Complete the text with the correct form of the verbs.

My friend Rory [1] *comes* (*come*) from Canada. He [2] .... (*live*) in Montreal. He [3] .... (*speak*) English and French. My French is awful, so he [4] .... (*not speak*) French to me. At the moment he's in England. He [5] .... (*stay*) with me for a month. But the weather isn't very good. It [6] .... (*rain*) again today, so we [7] .... (*spend*) the day at home. I [8] .... (*watch*) a football match on TV, but Rory [9] .... (*not watch*) it because he [10] .... (*not like*) football. Canadians [11] .... (*prefer*) ice hockey.

2 Past simple and past continuous

Work it out for yourself

A

A **Match sentences 1 and 2 with explanations a and b. Which sentence, 1 or 2, describes picture A?**

1 *At 7.15 Lucy **made** the dinner.* (past simple)

2 *At 7.15 Lucy **was making** the dinner.* (past continuous)

a She started to make the dinner before 7.15.

b She started to make the dinner at 7.15.

B

B **Look at picture B. Choose the right answer to the question.**

*What **was** Lucy **doing** when the face **appeared** at the window?*

1 She made the dinner when the face appeared.

2 She was making the dinner when the face appeared.

C **Match explanations 1 and 2 with sentences a and b.**

1 One action was in progress.

2 Another action interrupted it.

a The face appeared.

b She was making the dinner.

Check that you can

2.1 ● describe actions and situations in progress in the past.

Complete the sentences.

1 I cut my finger when I *was cleaning* (*clean*) my bike.

2 Their boat hit a whale when they .... (*sail*) to France.

3 Our English teacher got very angry because we .... (*not listen*).

4 I couldn't watch the film last night. Our television .... (*not work*).

5 I didn't hear the phone because everyone .... (*talk*).

6 The old man didn't see the 'Stop' sign because he .... (*not wear*) his glasses.

2.2 ● ask questions with the past continuous.

Make questions.

1 Where was he going?

1 I saw Harry at the station.
Where / he / go?

2 There were lots of policemen in the street.
What / they / do?

3 Helen was on the telephone for hours.
Who / she / phone?

4 I couldn't get an Internet connection on your computer.
Why / you / use / my computer?

Think of an answer to each question. Then ask and answer.

2.3 ● use the past simple and the past continuous.

Match 1–5 with a–e and make five sentences. Write the verbs in the past simple or the past continuous.

1e Megan was crying when she phoned me.

1 Megan (*cry*)

2 I (*do*) the shopping this morning

3 I (*not go*) into the living room

4 I (*shout*) at my brother

5 The passengers (*get*) ready for bed

a when I (*meet*) Gemma in the street.

b because my parents (*argue*).

c when the *Titanic* (*hit*) the iceberg.

d because he (*wear*) my new T-shirt.

e when she (*phone*) me.

Vocabulary and expressions

Visiting a new place
abroad
(to) be/feel homesick
(to) stay with (someone)

Greetings and introductions
Hi!/Hello!
How are you?
I'm fine, thanks.
This is Mrs Jones.
How do you do?
Nice to meet you.
Pleased to meet you.

Countries and nationalities
Argentina – Argentinian
Australia – Australian
Britain – British
Canada – Canadian
France – French
Greece – Greek
Italy – Italian
Japan – Japanese
Mexico – Mexican
Poland – Polish
Spain – Spanish
the USA – American

Language
as (a first language)
business
(to) communicate
(to) connect
culture
an English-speaking country
home page
international
worldwide

Numbers
a hundred
a thousand
a million
a billion
a quarter
one and a half
three quarters
two point seven five
per cent

Giving and accepting an apology
I'm sorry.
It's my fault. / It isn't my fault.
That's all right.
It doesn't matter.
Don't worry about it.

Verbs describing actions
(to) crash
(to) fall
(to) fly
(to) hit
(to) jump
(to) land
(to) sail
(to) sink

Adventure
arrow
bow
branch
(to) cut
exhausted
(to) fish
grass
hatchet
heart attack
knife
(to) shake
shelter (n.)
spear
survival
(to) survive
(the) wild

Link words
after
and
before
but
suddenly
then
when

Study skills 1 *Your coursebook*

Look through your book and find answers to these questions. You've got five minutes.

1 What do you like? What don't you like?
2 How many steps are there in each unit?
3 Is Step 3 the same as Steps 1 and 2?
4 In some of the activities you will learn new language. Find the names of at least two of these activities.
5 In some of the activities you will need to use the language for yourself. Find the names of some of these activities.
6 Look at the conversations with Ana in Steps 1 and 2. Where do you think they take place?
7 What is the theme of the Coursework?
8 If you don't understand a new word, what can you do?

Talk about your answers with the rest of the class.

How's it going?

• Your rating

Look again at pages 22 and 23. For each section decide on your rating: Good ✓✓✓ Not bad ✓✓
I can't remember much ✓

• Vocabulary

Choose two titles from the Vocabulary list, then close your book. How many words can you remember for each topic? Say the words and then write them on the board.

• Test a friend

Look again at Units 1 and 2. Think of at least two questions, then ask a friend.

What nationality is Ana?

What did Mark Taylor find?

• Correcting mistakes

Can you correct these mistakes? In some sentences there is more than one mistake.

1 ~~Ana like very much London.~~
Ana likes London very much.
2 ~~At the moment it rains outside.~~
3 ~~The last night I went to a restaurant.~~
4 ~~What time Jay did left his flat?~~
5 ~~I had a bath when my friend ringed me.~~

• Your Workbook

Complete the Learning Diaries for Units 1 and 2.

Coursework 1 My guidebook

Ana's making a guidebook about the UK. It's for other foreign students who are interested in visiting the UK in the future. This is her first page.

Read Ana's page about 'home life' in the UK, then make your own 'home life' page for a guidebook for visitors to your country. Write about your daily life, and about everyday life in general in your country.

Home life

If you stay with an English family, what will life be like? I don't know if the Grants are a typical English family, but I'll tell you about my life at their flat in north-west London.

During the week, the day starts at about 7.15. We have our breakfast in the kitchen. Tim and Penny Grant always have toast and coffee, but a lot of English people prefer tea. Charlie (Tim and Penny's son) has orange juice and cereal. If everyone is in a hurry, we don't have time to sit down. I often make a sandwich to take to the language school with me.

Tim and Penny leave the flat at about eight o'clock. They go to work on the tube. I get the bus to school. I usually walk to the bus stop with Charlie. A lot of British people travel to work by car. The roads are often very busy, especially during the 'rush hour' – the time when people go to work in the morning and go home at the end of the day.

We usually have our dinner together, but sometimes Penny works in the evening and sometimes Tim goes to the gym after work. We eat at about half past seven. After that, Tim reads the newspaper, Charlie does his homework and Penny watches TV or talks to her friends on the phone. We go to bed at about eleven.

At the weekend, Charlie and Tim sometimes go to a football match, and Tim always washes the car. Penny does the housework and Tim does the shopping at the supermarket near the flat. It's open nearly all the time and it's huge, with a big car park. Sometimes we go to the cinema, or we go for a walk on Hampstead Heath. Sometimes Tim and Penny's friends come to the flat for a meal, or just to say hello.

Tim likes DIY ('Do it yourself') and, at the moment, he's making some shelves for the bathroom. Penny often goes cycling at the weekend. Charlie spends a lot of time at his friend's flat, and he often argues with his parents when he doesn't help at home!

Module 2

Descriptions

In Module 2 Steps 1 and 2 you study

Grammar
- Comparatives and superlatives
- *(not) as ... as*
- Suggestions
- Expressions of quantity

Vocabulary
- Adjectives describing personality
- Names of places

Expressions
- Asking for a description
- Responding to suggestions

so that you can
- Give descriptions and make comparisons
- Describe differences and similarities
- Ask for descriptions
- Ask for, make and respond to suggestions
- Talk about a day out
- Talk about a place you know, and things you like and don't like there

In Step 3 you ...

read
- A personal Web page
- An article about a Japanese student's day

study
- Opposites: *un-* + adjective
- Uses of *get*
- Using pronouns and possessive adjectives
- Scanning

so that you can
- Write about yourself
- Write about a typical day

Life and culture

The British
Australia

Coursework 2

Part 2 Getting around
You write about interesting places in your country.

visits the cave under the castle.

From London, you can get to Cornwall by train or by coach. I went by coach. It takes quite a long time but it's much cheaper than the train.

Hyde Park
Hyde Park covers 140 ... It's a popular place fo... rugby, football and Fri... on the Serpentine, or ... just sit in a deckchair ... like Speakers' Corner ... about all sorts of diff...

I usually get the bus ... Hyde Park. If you live ... centre, you can get a ... or you can buy ticket... newsagent's, or you c... from the machine at t...

Brighton
Brighton is a fantastic place to go for the weekend. It's

What's it about?

What can you say about the pictures?

Now match the pictures with sentences 1–5.

1 Megan is taller than all her friends.
2 How about visiting Windsor Castle?
3 Carlos's hair isn't as curly as Clara's.
4 He's quite tall with light brown hair.
5 There are too many people – and too many goats!

a

b

c

d

e

3 People

STEP 1

In Step 1 you study
- comparatives and superlatives

so that you can
- give descriptions and make comparisons

1 Share your ideas

How many adjectives do you know to describe appearance?

blue

small

Can you describe the people at the bus stop?

The old woman is carrying a black umbrella. She's got a very small dog.

Remember!

Adjectives go before the noun:
She's got **long** hair. He's carrying a **big** plant.
The form of adjectives is always the same:
An **old** man. An **old** woman. Two **old** people.

2 Presentation

Everyone's shorter than me!

a Listen to Megan and follow in your book. Why is she different from her friends? Do you think she likes being different?

Megan McCarthy is 14. She lives in Leeds.

I'm 14, but I'm 1.83 metres tall. All my friends are shorter than me and I'm the tallest person in my family.

Everyone thinks I'm older than 14. On the bus, they think I'm an adult.

When I started secondary school, everyone stared at me. People were friendlier and more helpful at primary school. But it's easier now and I've got lots of mates.

Clothes are always a problem. I usually buy my clothes at a shop called *Long Tall Sally*, but they're more expensive than ordinary clothes. Shoes are even worse!

There are some advantages. I play basketball and people say I'm the best player in the school. And tall people often get better jobs and earn more money!

The most difficult thing is that I'm always different from other people. I just want to be the same as everyone else. But I'm tall and I'll always be tall, so I try to accept it and be positive about it.

b Read the text again. Match 1–8 with a–h and make true sentences.

1 Megan is taller
2 Megan's parents are shorter
3 She's the tallest person
4 People were friendlier
5 They were more
6 Her clothes are more
7 Megan always feels different
8 She wants to be the same

a from other people.
b helpful too.
c expensive than ordinary clothes.
d than her.
e when Megan was at primary school.
f as her friends.
g than her friends.
h in her family.

3 Key grammar
Comparatives and superlatives

Complete the sentences. How do you say these sentences in your language?

Megan's **taller** .... everyone else.
Her shoes are .... **expensive than** mine.
She's .... **tallest** person in her family.
They're **the** .... **expensive** shoes in the shop.

	Comparative	**Superlative**
Regular adjectives		
one syllable		
tall	taller	the tallest
two syllables with -y		
easy	easier	the easiest
two syllables		
helpful	more helpful	the most helpful
more than two syllables		
expensive	more expensive	the most expensive
Irregular adjectives		
good	better	the best
bad	worse	the worst

G 25

Remember!

She's different **from** her friends.
She wants to be the same **as** her friends.

4 Practice

a Make sentences with the comparative or superlative form of the adjectives in brackets.

1 *The longest* river in Africa is the Nile. (*long*)
2 London is *bigger than* Paris. (*big*)
3 Houses in London are .... houses in Leeds. (*expensive*)
4 Jay bought .... camera in the shop. (*cheap*)
5 Football is .... sport in Britain. (*popular*)
6 Justin Gatlin was .... runner in the race last night. (*fast*)
7 He was .... all the others. (*good*)
8 I think basketball is .... football. (*exciting*)
9 You must be .... (*careful*)

b Write sentences about some of the girls in Megan's basketball team. Use comparatives and superlatives. How many sentences can you make? You've got three minutes!

Tessa is the most positive. Sara is older than Shereen.

Name	Age	Height	Positive attitude
Becky	14	1.62m	*
Tessa	13	1.58m	*****
Sara	15	1.65m	***
Jenny	16	1.67m	**
Shereen	14	1.72m	****

c **Test a friend** Ask at least one question about the girls.

Is Jenny older or younger than Shereen?

She's older.

d **What about you?** Describe a friend. Use comparatives and superlatives.

My best friend is Samira. She's older than me. She's the kindest person in the class.

5 Writing and speaking
Can you guess?

Use what you know

Write a description of a thing, an animal, a person or a place, using comparatives and superlatives. Read it to a friend. Can your friend find the answer?

It's faster than a bike but it's slower than a train. It isn't a car. It begins with 'b'.

A bus!

Try this!

How many adjectives can you find?

ATALLIKINDSTAFRIENDLYOUSHORTOLDTOBLACKBUSOPTIMISTICMECRAZYTELYOUNG

STEP 2

In Step 2 you study
- adjectives describing personality
- *(not) as ... as*
- asking for a description

so that you can
- describe differences and similarities
- ask for and give descriptions

1 Key vocabulary *Adjectives describing personality*

a Match each adjective with a description. You've got three minutes!

adventurous clever confident
easy-going generous
hard-working independent
lazy moody shy

1 I like doing things on my own. I don't like asking for help.
2 I'm sometimes in a bad mood and sometimes in a good mood.
3 One day I want to climb Mount Everest.
4 I spend a lot of time on my school work.
5 I enjoy staying in bed and watching TV.
6 I usually get good marks in my exams and I can speak three different languages.
7 I try to give my friends nice birthday presents and I like sharing things.
8 I don't like meeting new people and I hate going to parties.
9 I don't often worry and I never really get angry.
10 I'm not shy. I'm happy to be me.

Listen and check.

b **What about you?** Make at least two sentences about your personality.

I don't like meeting new people. I'm not very confident. I'm quite moody.

2 Key pronunciation *Stress in words*

Match the adjectives in Exercise 1 with these stress patterns.

1 ●•●• *easy-going*
2 •●••
3 ••●•
4 •●•
5 ●••
6 ●•
7 ●

Listen, check and say the words.

3 Presentation *What are they like?*

a Look at the photo, then listen to the conversation and follow in your book. Who is:

1 the boy on the left? 2 the girl in the middle?
3 the girl on the right?

Ana's showing Jay some photos of her friends and family.

JAY: Who's that, in the middle? Is that your sister?
ANA: Yes, that's Clara.
JAY: Is she older or younger than you?
ANA: She's older. I'm 18 and she's 21. Er ... how old are you, Jay?
JAY: Me? Oh, I'm 18 ... well, nearly 18. Anyway, what about the others?
ANA: That's my best friend, on the right. Her name's Emilia. She's really nice.
JAY: And who's that, on the left? Is that your brother?
ANA: No, that's Clara's boyfriend, Carlos. He's quite shy, but he's very clever.
JAY: So what's your brother like?
ANA: Julio? He's great. He's really easy-going. But he annoys me sometimes. He's so lazy!
JAY: What does he look like? Does he look like you?
ANA: Yes, a bit. His hair isn't as curly as mine, but we've got the same colour eyes and the same nose.
JAY: But is he as good-looking as you?
ANA: Pardon?
JAY: Oh, er ... nothing. Er, have you got any photos of Veracruz?

b Are these sentences true or false? Correct the false sentences.

1 Ana is older than Clara.
2 Jay isn't as old as Ana.
3 Clara's best friend is called Emilia.
4 Ana's brother isn't in the photo.
5 Carlos is a confident person.
6 Ana's brother is quite moody.
7 Julio is very hard-working.
8 Ana looks a bit like her brother.
9 Ana's hair is curlier than her brother's.

4 Key grammar (not) as ... as

Complete the examples and read the explanation.

> His hair isn't .... curly **as** mine.
> Is Carlos **as** friendly .... Julio?
> *We use* as + *adjective* + as *to talk about differences and similarities.*

G → 26

5 Practice

a Make questions using *as ... as*. Then ask a friend for his/her opinion.

1 maths / hard / physics
2 tennis / exciting / football
3 flying / dangerous / travelling by car
4 cats / intelligent / dogs
5 boys / moody / girls

Is maths as hard as physics?

I think physics is harder than maths.

b **Test a friend** Write a sentence with *as ... as* but leave a blank. Can your friend complete the sentence?

Paris isn't as ... as London.

Paris isn't as big as London.

6 Key expressions *Asking for a description*

Match the questions with the answers. How do you say the questions in your language?

1 Does Jay look like his father?
2 What does Jay look like?
3 What's Jay like?

a He's quite tall, with light brown hair.
b He's an independent person, and he's very generous.
c Yes, he does. They've both got the same nose and eyes.

Listen and check.

7 Listening and speaking *Personality test*

a Which shape do you prefer? Write the name.

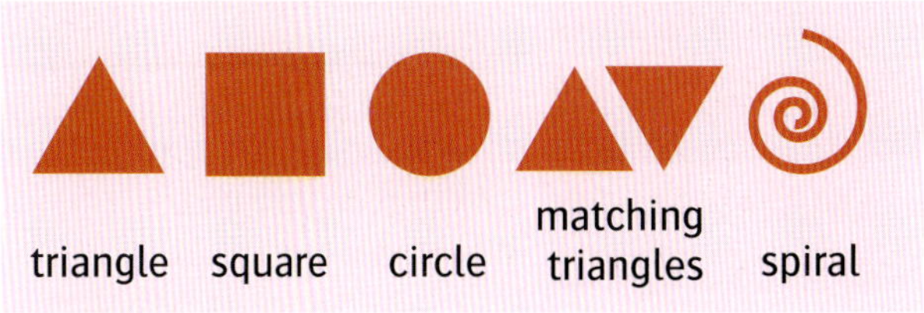

b Jay is interviewing five friends. Listen and match each person with the shape they prefer.

Martin *triangle* Helen Mike Fiona Lizzie

c Listen again. There are two adjectives for each shape. Copy and complete the list.

triangle	*shy*	....
spiral	....	*adventurous*
matching triangles	*friendly*	....
square	*honest*	....
circle	....	*generous*

d **What about you?** Describe yourself.

I chose the spiral. I don't think the test is right because I'm not very adventurous.

8 Writing and speaking *People I know*

Use what you know

Write about someone you know. Which shape do you think matches his/her personality? What's he/she like?

I think my friend David matches the square, because he's very easy-going. He never gets angry.

Now tell a friend about him/her.

STEP 3

In Step 3 you
- read a personal Web page
- study opposites: *un-* + adjective

so that you can
- write about yourself

1 Share your ideas
The Internet

How many Internet words do you know?

Web page | click

2 Reading

a Read the text. What do you think of Daniel's Web page?

Daniel Trent's Web page

http://www.daniel-trent.net/

Daniel Trent's Web page

- What's new?
- Joke page
- My pictures
- Favorite* places
- Family fun
- My diary
- Links
- Contact me

Welcome to my Web page.

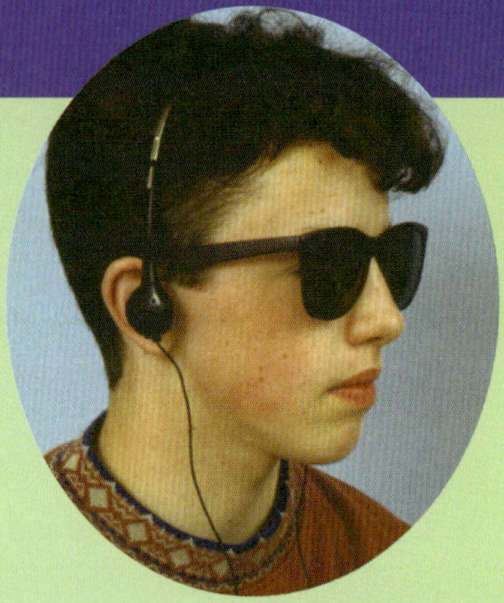

About me
I'm 15 years old and I have* black hair and brown eyes. I'm quite short. My friends say I look cool in these sunglasses. What do you think?

My school
I'm a student at Bay High School in Florida. It only takes five minutes to get to school because I live nearby. There are thirty students in my class. I'm quite good at biology and art. My worst subject is history.

My home
I live in an apartment* on the seventh floor. I can see a river from my bedroom window. My mother often gets annoyed with me – she says my room is always untidy.

My friends
My best friends are Simon and Nathan. Nathan is a bit shy, and Simon is very easy-going. I look like Simon. People often think we're brothers. Last weekend we went to SeaWorld, in Orlando. It's amazing!

FAST FACTS

Favorite movie	The Matrix. I love adventure movies* and Keanu Reeves is my favorite* actor. He's the greatest!
Sports	I'm captain of my school tennis team. Last year we won a big competition. Click here to see the photos.
Music	I like Beyoncé. I have* all her CDs. She's one of the most popular singers in the US.
Most embarrassing moment	Two months ago I was shopping in Fort Lauderdale with Simon when we thought we saw Beyoncé. I shouted and ran after her but, when she turned round, it wasn't her. I felt so stupid!

* American English	British English
I have black hair.	I've got black hair.
apartment	flat
favorite	favourite
movie	film

b Comprehension check

Read the text again. For each sentence write T (true), F (false) or ? (the text doesn't say).

1. Daniel lives in the USA.
2. He likes his biology teacher.
3. He's better at history than biology.
4. His bedroom is very tidy.
5. Daniel looks like his brother.
6. His brother's name is Simon.
7. Daniel's a good tennis player.
8. Two months ago he met Beyoncé.

c Reading skills *Using pronouns and possessive adjectives*

Find these sentences in the text. Read the sentence before. What do the underlined words refer to?

1 my = Daniel's

1. Welcome to my Web page.
2. She says my room is always untidy.
3. People often think we're brothers.
4. It's amazing!
5. He's the greatest!
6. Last year we won a big competition.
7. I have all her CDs.
8. We thought we saw Beyoncé.
9. I ran after her.

3 Word work *Opposites un- + adjective*

a Read the two lists of adjectives and make pairs of opposites.

untidy	unfriendly
moody	lazy
confident	easy-going
friendly	clever
hard-working	unpopular
stupid	tidy
popular	shy

b To make the opposite of some adjectives, we add *un-* at the beginning.

tidy **un**tidy   popular **un**popular

Look at these adjectives. Which one doesn't form its opposite using *un-*?

healthy kind lucky necessary boring comfortable happy

Writing guide *Writing a Web page*

- Choose a title.
  Marco Rosafio's Web page.
- Write an introduction.
  This Web page is all about me.
- Make a list of topics.
  All about me
  My school
  My friends
- Give more details.
  I usually meet my friends at the weekend.
  We often go to ...
- Add some more information.
  'Fast facts'
  Favourite book: My favourite book is ...

4 Writing *A Web page*

Use what you know

Write the text for your own Web page.
Write at least two sentences for each topic.

All about me
How old are you?
What do you look like?
What are you like?

My school
What's the name of your school?
Where is it?
What are your best/worst subjects?

My home
Where do you live?
Describe your room.

My friends
Who are your best friends?
What are they like?

Fast facts
What are your interests?
What sort of films/music/sports do you like?
Who are your favourite stars?

Extra exercises

1 Complete the conversation. Choose from a–h.

A: What's your brother like? Is he shy?

B: [1] c

A: What does he look like?

B: [2] ....

A: What about your sister? Does she look like you?

B: [3] ....

A: Is she very moody?

B: [4] ....

A: Is she as nice as you?

B: [5] ....

a They're short, with long, fair hair.
b Yes, a bit, but I've got darker hair.
c No, he's very confident.
d He likes football.
e She doesn't look like my brother.
f No, of course not! I'm the nicest person in my family!
g He's tall, with dark curly hair.
h Well, not very, but she's moodier than me.

2 Choose the right words.

1 Tom's hair is .... mine.
   a as long as
   b long as
   c longer
2 The weather in England was bad but in Scotland it was ....
   a bad
   b worse
   c worst
3 These old trainers are .... shoes I've got.
   a most comfortable
   b the most comfortable
   c comfortable than
4 Mark's school is different .... an ordinary school.
   a as
   b with
   c from
5 Our teacher says English is .... than French, but I don't agree.
   a more easy
   b easier
   c easiest

3 Put the letters in the right order and make six adjectives. Then use the adjectives to complete the sentences.

NTECDIFNO LYZA EITLGNELITN ORSGUEEN AURSDUTONEV ODOYM

1 My sister's more .... than me. She always gets better marks in exams.
2 Tim's very .... He bought everyone a watch for Christmas.
3 The students in this class aren't very hard-working. In fact, they're ....
4 My friends and I are quite .... We like new and exciting things.
5 You're very .... sometimes, especially when your football team loses!
6 I fell off my bike last month and now I don't feel very .... when I cycle.

4 Complete the sentences. Use comparatives or superlatives, or *as ... as*.

1 Simon likes maths but I think history is .... (*interesting*)
2 Jane's .... student in her class. (*good*)
3 I think that biology is .... chemistry. They're both really hard! (*difficult*)
4 My friend David is one of .... people in the school. (*lazy*)
5 I like Mr Jones, our physics teacher, because he's .... the other teachers. (*friendly*)

5 Complete the conversation. Use your imagination.

A: I'm looking for Michael. Can you see him?

B: I don't know him. What does he look like?

A: He ....

B: Is he your brother?

A: No, he's my pen friend.

B: Oh, really. What's he like?

A: He ....

6 How do you say these sentences in your language?

1 I've got lots of mates.
2 Do you look like your father?
3 What's the weather like?
4 They've got the same eyes.
5 What does he look like?
6 I look cool in these sunglasses.

Extra reading

Life and culture

The British

When you think about Britain and British people, what do you imagine?

'When people think about Britain, they probably think of England – the Royal Family, the Tower of London and Buckingham Palace. But there's also Scotland and Wales! Scottish and Welsh people are very proud of their country and nationality. When people ask me where I come from, I always say I'm Scottish.'

Ewan McDonald, Edinburgh

'I think people sometimes imagine that we all live in beautiful houses in the country. Well, my aunt lives on a farm, but these days houses in the country can be very expensive. Most people live in towns, but it's true that houses are more common than flats. And houses in Britain nearly always have a garden. British people love gardening!'

Susan Phillips, Manchester

'Foreigners think that Britain is cold and it rains all the time. This isn't true! We often have great summers here. The best weather is in the south and, in the summer, the beaches near my home are always busy.'

Kevin Ribson, Brighton

'We definitely don't have tea and sandwiches every day at five o'clock! But when we're on holiday in Cornwall, we sometimes have a 'cream tea' – scones, jam and cream. Delicious! And it's true that you can find some fantastic cakes here – my favourite is chocolate cake.'

Uzma Jones, Cardiff

'People think that a lot of British people are hooligans – we have a bad reputation at football matches. It's true that some young people behave badly, but most of us are friendly and quite polite – just like young people in other countries.'

Samuel Jakes, Liverpool

ABOUT THE BRITISH

Tea was popular in China nearly five thousand years ago, but it didn't arrive in Britain until 1652. Now British people drink an average of three cups of tea a day.

Task

Read the texts, then copy and complete the table. Add your own ideas.

What do foreigners imagine when they think of Britain?

Places to visit: *Buckingham Palace ...*
Food:
People:
Homes:
Weather:

Do you know what foreigners imagine when they think of your country?

4 Places

STEP 1

In Step 1 you study
- names of places and buildings
- suggestions
- responding to suggestions

so that you can
- ask for, make and respond to suggestions
- talk about a day out

1 Key vocabulary *Places*

Match the words with the photos and complete the descriptions. You've got two minutes!

theme park castle art gallery temple stadium department store mosque

1 The Olympic .... in Athens
2 The Tate Modern, an .... in London
3 The Ginkakuji .... in Kyoto
4 Windsor .... , near London
5 The Blue .... in Istanbul
6 Disneyworld in Florida, the world's first ....
7 Selfridges, a .... in Oxford Street, London

Listen and check.

2 Presentation *Shall we go out?*

a What can you say about the photos?

b Listen and follow in your book. Why isn't it easy to make a plan?

Ana's talking to Jay and his friends. It's Saturday tomorrow and they want to go out somewhere together.

JAY: Shall we go out somewhere tomorrow?
ANA: That's a nice idea. What shall we do?
JAY: How about visiting Windsor Castle?
ANA: That's fine with me.
LIZZIE: I'd rather go shopping. Shall we go to Oxford Street?
MARTIN: No! Why don't we go on the London Eye?
JAY: I don't really want to do that. Anyway, it's very expensive.
MARTIN: Well, how about taking a boat trip on the Thames?
JAY: Yes, OK. Let's take a boat trip. I think that's a good idea.
ANA: I don't mind. How about you, Lizzie?
LIZZIE: Well, I'd rather look round the shops really ... but yes, all right then.
JAY: Good! So what time shall we meet?
LIZZIE: Hang on! There's a new exhibition at the Tate Modern. Why don't we go to that?
JAY: Lizzie! I think we've got enough suggestions!

c Read the conversation again. Find:

1 five things you can do in or near London.
2 seven different suggestions.

d Are these sentences true or false? Correct the false sentences.

1 Jay wants to visit Windsor Castle.
2 Ana doesn't agree with Jay's suggestion.
3 Lizzie doesn't want to go shopping.
4 Martin makes two suggestions.
5 Jay wants to go on the London Eye.
6 Ana suggests a trip on the Thames.
7 They decide to go on a boat trip.
8 Lizzie agrees, but she really wants to go shopping.
9 Lizzie hasn't got any other suggestions.

3 Key grammar *Suggestions*

Look at the conversation again, then complete the examples.

Asking for suggestions

Where / What time | .... we | go? / meet?

Making suggestions

Shall / Why .... | we | go to Oxford Street?

Let's .... a boat trip.
How .... visiting Windsor Castle?

We use Shall we ...?, Why don't we ...?, Let's ..., How about + -ing ...? *to make suggestions.*

G 22

4 Practice

a Match 1–8 with a–h and make complete sentences.

1 Shall we go	a we meet? Is 7.30 all right?
2 How about	b a policeman?
3 What time shall	c shall we have our lunch?
4 Let's	d postcards.
5 Why don't we ask	e we sit down?
6 Where	f buy a map.
7 Let's buy some	g on the bus or the tube?
8 Shall	h going to the Tate Modern?

b **Test a friend** Write a suggestion and then put the words in the wrong order. Swap with a friend. Write his/her sentence.

A: Castle / to / go / shall / Windsor / tomorrow / we ?
B: Shall we go to Windsor Castle tomorrow?

Try this!
Find six more places.
UMEMSU ATETREH TACERDHAL
AEMNIC ALCPEA UMUQARAI

5 Key expressions
Responding to suggestions

Match sentences 1–7 with explanations a–d.

1 That's a nice idea.
2 I don't mind.
3 I'd rather (go shopping).
4 I don't really want to do that.
5 That's fine with me.
6 I think that's a good idea.
7 All right then.

a OK, I agree.
b No, I don't agree.
c I've got a different idea and I prefer that.
d It isn't important to me. You can choose.

6 Key pronunciation /k/ /p/ /t/

a Listen and say these words.

1 /k/ park mosque picnic
2 /p/ trip map shop
3 /t/ art street boat

b Now listen to some more words and repeat. Is the sound 1, 2 or 3?

7 Speaking *A day out*

Use what you know

Work in a group. Imagine you want to go out together for the day. Choose a town/city: your home town, your capital city, London.

Make at least one suggestion: *Why don't we go to Buckingham Palace?*

Respond to your friends' ideas: *I don't mind. / That's fine with me.*

Find a place that you all want to visit.

STEP 2

In Step 2 you study

- expressions of quantity

so that you can

- talk about a place you know, and things you like and don't like there

1 Share your ideas

What do you know about Australia? Look at the tourist brochure for Lightning Ridge. What can you say about Lightning Ridge?

> The weather in the centre of Australia is hot and dry.

> There isn't much rain in Lightning Ridge.

2 Presentation *Too many tourists!*

a Listen and follow in your book. Are Cody and Dee describing things they like, or things they don't like?

> My name's Brett Scoble and I live in Lightning Ridge. I think it's great but my grandad and my sister don't always agree!

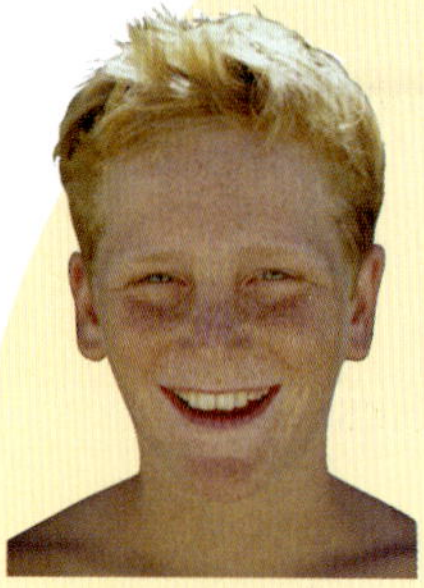
Brett

Cody

> Lightning Ridge is usually a nice quiet town. But every Easter, hundreds of visitors come here for the goat races. It's terrible! There's too much traffic and there's too much noise. There are too many people – and too many goats!

Dee

> I think it's boring here. There are a lot of sports facilities, I suppose. But, for me, there isn't enough to do. There aren't enough places for young people and there aren't enough good shops. I'd rather live in a bigger town, but I'm a student so I haven't got enough money at the moment. But it isn't all bad. And if you like poisonous snakes, it's the perfect place for you!

b Read the texts again. Match 1–9 with a–i and make true sentences.

1. At Easter, there are always a
2. There are a lot
3. Cody says it's very
4. He thinks there are
5. There isn't usually
6. Dee thinks Lightning Ridge
7. She says there
8. There aren't many
9. Dee hasn't got

a places for young people.
b noisy at Easter.
c much traffic in Lightning Ridge.
d lot of visitors.
e much money.
f of cars too.
g is boring.
h too many visitors.
i isn't enough to do.

3 Key grammar
Expressions of quantity

Read the examples and complete the explanation with *too many* and *enough*.

There's **too much** noise.
There are **too many** visitors.
There's **a lot of** traffic.
There are **a lot of** sports facilities.
She hasn't got **enough** money.
There aren't **enough** good shops.

We use too much *with uncountable nouns and* .... *with countable nouns.*
We can use .... *and* a lot of *with countable and uncountable nouns.*

G 23, 24

4 Practice

a Complete the sentences with *too much, too many, a lot of* or *enough*.

1 He's got .... goats!
2 There are .... people in the car.
3 They haven't got .... food.
4 He's got .... ketchup on his chips.
5 There aren't .... seats for everyone.

b **What about you?** Think of at least two things you like or don't like about school.

We do a lot of sport. I enjoy that. But we have too many English lessons. We don't do enough music.

5 Listening *It's a fantastic place!*

a Listen to Brett talking about Lightning Ridge. How does he feel about living there?

b Listen again and choose the right answer.

1 Lightning Ridge has got ...
  a a five-star golf course. b a big swimming pool.
  c three theme parks.
2 Brett and his friends go to the Water Theme Park ...
  a before school. b two or three times in the summer.
  c after school in the summer.
3 In his school holidays, Brett works ...
  a as an artist. b at a caravan park. c at an art gallery.
4 Brett likes ...
  a the wildlife. b the trees and flowers. c the crocodiles.
5 In the evening, Brett's family often ...
  a eat in their neighbours' garden. b eat outside.
  c eat at their neighbours' house.

c How many true sentences can you make about Lightning Ridge? Use these words.

art galleries artists rain trees and flowers wildlife
rare birds different nationalities friendly people

1 There isn't much ...
2 There aren't many ...
3 There's a lot of ...
4 There are a lot of ...

6 Writing and speaking *A place I know*

Use what you know

Describe your village or town or your capital city.

Where is it? What are the things you like or don't like?
Use: *a lot of, too much/many, not enough.* Talk about your ideas with the class and then write a description.

There are a lot of good shops. There aren't enough parks.

STEP 3

In Step 3 you
- read an article about a Japanese student's day
- study the verb *get*

so that you can
- write about a typical day

1 Share your ideas
Student life

What do you know about life in Japan? Do you think the students there have an easier or a harder life than you?

I'm not sure, but I think Japanese students work really hard.

2 Reading

a Reading skills *Scanning*

Read the text quickly and find answers to these questions. Don't read every word. You've got three minutes!

1 What time do lessons start in Japan?
2 How much time do students have for lunch?
3 What time do lessons finish?
4 Are extra evening classes popular?

One World Magazine

It's a hard life!

Yesterday was a normal schoolday for Yumiko, a fourteen-year-old student at Higashi High School in Tokyo, Japan.

At 6.15 am, while you were probably still asleep, Yumiko was getting ready for school. She did some homework then, at 7.30, she left home and travelled for an hour by train to get to school. Her first class started at 8.40. She had four lessons in the morning, and she sat in the same seat all the time. In Japan, students stay in the same classroom and wait for their teacher.

There isn't a cafeteria or a canteen at Yumiko's school so, at 12.30, she stayed in her classroom with her classmates and ate her packed lunch. She had 50 minutes for lunch and then had two more classes.

At 3 pm classes finished and it was time for *o shoji*. This is when the students clean the school. Yumiko helped to tidy the classroom and, after that, she went to baseball club and practised for two hours. Every student in Japan goes to a club after school. Some of the clubs, like Yumiko's baseball club, even meet every Saturday and Sunday as well.

After baseball, Yumiko had a burger and then took a 30-minute train journey to a special school called a *juku*. She stayed there for three hours, studying for her exams. Yumiko likes going to *juku* because she says it's more fun than normal school, and more interesting. Her parents don't mind paying because they hope it will help her to get into a good university. About 60% of Japanese high school students take these extra classes. Finally, Yumiko went home and did another hour's homework before she went to bed – at midnight.

And you thought *you* had a hard life!

b Comprehension check Listen, and read the text again. Then read these sentences about Yumiko's day. Put them in the right order.

1i

a She had her lunch.
b Her lessons started at 8.40 and finished at 12.30.
c She played baseball.
d She got ready for school.
e After that, she had two more classes.
f At twelve o'clock she finally went to bed.
g She got the train at 7.35 am.
h She ate a burger on her way to the station.
i She got up at 6 am.
j Then she helped to clean the school.
k She went to her evening classes.

c What do you think of Yumiko's life? Share your opinions.

> I think she has too many classes.

3 Word work get

a Complete the sentences with the words in the box.

get (x2) get up get to get on get off get into (x2) get out of get dressed get ready get home

1 I usually .... at seven, but on Sunday I stay in bed all morning.
2 Yumiko wants to .... a good university.
3 I always have a snack when I .... from school.
4 This is our station. Quick! We must ....
5 Hurry up and .... for school! Have you got all your books?
6 Every summer, Brett and his friend Zak .... a job at the Crocodile Caravan Park.
7 We must go. Go outside and .... the car.
8 Mr and Mrs Grant leave the house at eight and they .... work at half past eight.
9 'How can they escape?' 'They can .... the window.'
10 I sometimes .... the bus to the town centre but, when I've got enough time, I walk.
11 They have a shower in the morning before they ....
12 .... the train and find some seats! It's leaving in a minute.

b How do you say these different verbs with *get* in your language?

c Test a friend Write a sentence in your language using one of the verbs in 3a. Can your friend translate it into English?

Remember!

She **goes home** on the train.
She **gets home** at ten thirty.
We don't say ~~goes/gets to home~~.

Writing guide *Planning your writing*

- Think of some ideas. Write notes about the most important events of the day.
  good film on TV lost my jacket
- Organise your ideas. Put the events in the right order.
  I didn't hear my alarm clock so I got up late.
- Use link words.
  After that I ... Then ... ... so I ...
- Add some details. Write about your feelings and opinions.
  I was really angry.
- Check your spelling and punctuation. Look for other mistakes. Then write a final version.

4 Writing *A typical day*

Use what you know

Write about a day in your life or about an imaginary day in a different place.

What time did you get up?
What did you do?
Where did you go?
Who were you with?
Did you have any problems?
How did you feel?

Extra exercises

1 Complete the conversations. Use *one* word.

1 A: We haven't got much food in the fridge.
B: Well, how .... going to a restaurant?
2 A: Where do you want to stay in London?
B: .... don't we stay at a bed and breakfast? It's cheaper than a hotel.
3 A: .... we look round the shops?
B: That's a good idea. I need to buy a sweater.
4 A: ....'s go to Scotland this summer.
B: Yes. I'd love to see Edinburgh Castle.
5 A: What time .... we meet on Friday night?
B: About eight o'clock, outside the cinema.

2 Complete the conversations.

1 Let's eat in the cafeteria at lunchtime.
a I'd rather meet at lunchtime.
b No, I'm not.
c That's fine with me.

2 Do you want to watch a film tonight?
a All right, then.
b I like your watch.
c No. I don't really want to watch sport.

3 Shall we invite Mark and Wendy for dinner at the weekend?
a OK. I'm free on Thursday.
b Yes, that's a good idea.
c How about you?

4 Would you like tea or coffee?
a All right, then.
b I don't mind.
c Not really.

5 Why don't we take a boat trip on the Thames?
a I think I'd rather go to the Tate Modern.
b What's the time?
c I'd prefer to take a boat trip.

3 Complete the sentences with the names of places or buildings.

1 If you want to see some old paintings, go to an art g.......... .
2 Old Trafford is a fabulous football s.......... in Manchester.
3 A c.......... is a large, important church.
4 Disneyland is one of the best t.......... parks in the world.
5 Kings and queens usually live in a p.......... .
6 You can see lots of fish when you visit an a.......... .
7 A lot of Muslims go to a m.......... five times a day.
8 Harrods is a famous d.......... store in London.

4 Read the text and choose the right words for each space.

Last Saturday night I ate too [1].......... food and I got bad stomach ache. I went to bed late so I didn't get [2].......... sleep. The next morning I looked in the fridge but there [3].......... enough milk for breakfast. I decided to go to the shops, but it was Sunday and [4].......... the shops were closed. I found a shop, but when I looked in my purse, I didn't have [5].......... money to pay for my shopping, so I went home and fell asleep!

1	a many	b enough	c much
2	a lot	b enough	c many
3	a weren't	b didn't	c wasn't
4	a nearly all	b much	c a lot
5	a enough	b many	c lot of

5 Complete the second sentence so that it means the same as the first one. Use a verb and *too much, too many* or *not ... enough.*

1 Sue's tired. She slept for only three hours last night.
Sue *didn't have enough* sleep last night.
2 There were hundreds of people at the party. It was awful!
There .... people at the party.
3 Our teacher gave us a lot of homework and I can't finish it this evening.
Our teacher .... homework.
4 I want to buy this belt but it costs €10.00, and I've only got €8.00.
I .... money.
5 This book has got over 900 pages.
This book .... pages.

6 How do you say these sentences in your language?

1 I don't mind.
2 That's a nice idea.
3 Anyway, it's very expensive.
4 Yes, all right, then.
5 I haven't got enough time.
6 That's fine with me.

Extra reading

Life and culture

Australia

Who were the first Australians? What do you know about the first European settlers?

Australia is the sixth largest country in the world. Eighty-five per cent of people live in the big cities, so you can travel for thousands of kilometres and never see anyone. Outside the cities, the land in Australia is mainly hot desert. This is called the outback. In some parts of the outback, there aren't any schools. So children learn from the *School of the Air* – by radio, email and television. And when people in the outback are ill, their doctor visits them by plane – the 'Flying Doctor'.

The first Australians were Aboriginals. They lived in Australia 50,000 years before the Europeans. When the Europeans arrived, they killed many Aboriginals and took their land. Today, only one per cent of the population are Aboriginals, and many of them live in the cities.

The first British ships arrived in Botany Bay in 1788 – they were 'prison ships' and the first settlers were convicts. Australia's first police force was a group of twelve of the best-behaved convicts! Later, immigrants from other European countries started to arrive. Today, nearly 25% of Australians were born in another country. The main language of Australia is English but there are also a lot of Italian, Greek, Cantonese and Arabic speakers.

Australia produces a lot of the world's wool – about 70%. It's important to protect the sheep from dingoes (wild dogs), so there is a fence called the 'dingo fence'. It's 1.8 metres high and 5,531 kilometres long – and it's the world's longest fence.

Statistics

- 7,682,300 km^2
- 20m people
- 24m cows
- 40m kangaroos
- 150m sheep

Climate July and August are the coldest months. Many Australians go skiing!

Biggest city Sydney is the biggest city, but Canberra is the capital.

National day Australia Day (26th January) is the day when the British arrived in 1788.

Famous for Australian football, swimming, rugby, cricket, wine, films

Currency The currency is the Australian dollar.

Task

Read the text, then copy and complete the fact file.

Fact file	
Country: *Australia*	Original inhabitants:
Population:	Currency:
Capital city:	Coldest months:
Main language:	Important dates:

Now complete a fact file for your country.

ABOUT AUSTRALIA

There are over 500,000 camels in Australia. In 1840 explorers brought camels with them to help them in their journey across the desert.

Module 2 Review

Grammar check

1 Comparatives and superlatives

Work it out for yourself

A Match these adjectives with descriptions a–d: *expensive, long, modern, curly, short.*

a an adjective with one syllable
b an adjective with two syllables ending in *-y*
c an adjective with two syllables
d an adjective with more than two syllables

B Look at the three lines.

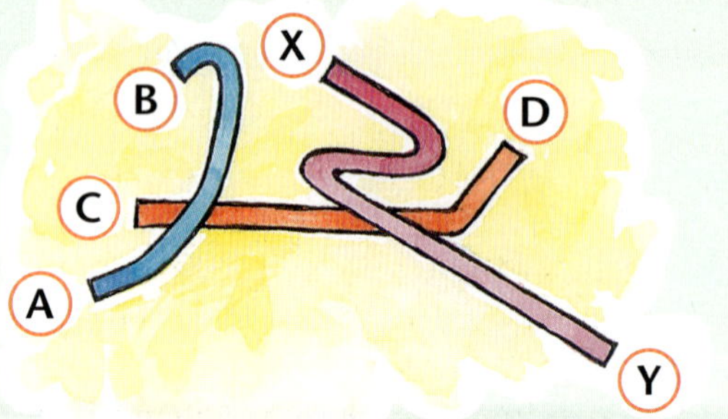

Answer the questions.

1 Is AB shorter than CD?
2 Is XY curlier than CD?
3 Is CD as long as XY?
4 Is AB as curly as XY?
5 Which is the longest line?
6 Which is the curliest line?

Look at the three clocks.

Answer the questions.

7 Is B more modern than A?
8 Is C as expensive as B?
9 Which is the most expensive clock?

C Match 1–4 with a–d and make four explanations.

1 For adjectives with one syllable ...
2 For most adjectives with two or more syllables ...
3 For adjectives with two syllables ending in *-y* ...
4 For all adjectives ...

a we put *more* before the adjective for the comparative, and *the most* for the superlative.
b we use *as* + adjective + *as* to say that things or people are the same.
c we add *-er* or *-r* for the comparative, and *the* + *-est* or *-st* for the superlative.
d we take out *-y* and add *-ier* for the comparative, and *the* + *-iest* for the superlative.

Check that you can

1.1 • make comparisons.

Rewrite the sentences in a different way, without changing the meaning. Use the comparative form of the adjectives.

1 Clara's hair is longer than Ana's.

1 Ana's hair isn't as long as Clara's.
2 CDs aren't as expensive as DVDs.
3 Rhinoceroses aren't as heavy as elephants.
4 Boys aren't often as confident as girls.
5 Gemma isn't as moody as Kirsty.
6 My brother isn't as easy-going as me.

1.2 • use superlative forms.

Complete the questions. Use the superlative form of the adjectives in brackets.

1 How old is *the oldest* man in the world? (*old*)
2 What is .... animal in the world? (*large*)
3 What is .... sport in the USA? (*popular*)
4 What is .... thing you've got? (*useful*)
5 Who is .... person in your family? (*happy*)
6 What is .... subject for you at school? (*difficult*)

Answer the questions if you can.

2 Irregular forms

Work it out for yourself

What are the missing adjectives?

Adjective	Comparative	Superlative
....	better	the best
....	worse	the worst

Check that you can

- use *better, the best, worse, the worst.*

Complete the text.

We had a French exam last week. I got 52%. Jack's mark was [1] better than mine. He got 65%. I wasn't pleased because I think I'm [2].......... at French than Jack. Lucy got [3].......... mark in the class. She got 83%. Sally got [4].......... mark. She only got 21%. She had a headache during the exam, and her headache was [5].......... when she got her result!

3 Making suggestions

Work it out for yourself

Look at these four ways of making a suggestion. Why is sentence 3 different?

1 *Why don't we go into town?*
2 *Shall we go into town?*
3 *How about going into town?*
4 *Let's go into town.*

Check that you can

- make suggestions.

It's Saturday afternoon. You're asking your friends: *What shall we do?* Write their suggestions. Use the verbs in the box.

watch go get make have look round have play

1 *Why don't we have a coffee at Café Rouge?*

1 a coffee at Café Rouge (*Why ...?*)
2 cards (*Shall ...?*)
3 a bus into town (*Let's ...*)
4 to the bowling alley (*How ...?*)
5 the shops (*Let's ...*)
6 the tennis final on TV (*Why ...?*)
7 a barbecue in the garden (*How ...?*)
8 a packed lunch and go to the beach (*Shall ...?*)

4 Expressions of quantity

Work it out for yourself

Read the explanations and the examples. Then answer the questions.

Uncountable nouns are things we can't count: *pasta, music, bread.*

Countable nouns are things we can count: *books, songs, friends.*

a lot of *pasta*	=	a big amount of pasta
a lot of *books*	=	a big number of books
too much *pasta*	=	more than the right amount of pasta
too many *books*	=	more than the right number of books
enough *pasta*	=	the right amount of pasta
enough *books*	=	the right number of books

1 Do we use *too much* or *too many* with uncountable nouns?
2 Do we use *too much* or *too many* with countable nouns?
3 Can we use *a lot of* with countable and uncountable nouns?
4 Can we use *enough* with countable and uncountable nouns?
5 Does *a lot of* mean the same as *too much / too many?*

Check that you can

- use *a lot of, too much/too many, enough.*

Complete the sentences.

1 She's got .... bottles.
2 There are .... bottles.
3 There's .... water in the bath.
4 There's .... water for everyone, but there aren't .... glasses.

Vocabulary and expressions

Adjectives describing personality
adventurous
clever
confident
easy-going
friendly
generous
hard-working
honest
independent
lazy
moody
popular
shy
stupid
tidy
unfriendly
unkind
unpopular
untidy

Asking for a description
Does he look like his father?
What's he like?
What does he look like?
He looks like his father.

The Internet
(to) click (on)
(to) connect
home page
links
Web page

Places
aquarium
art gallery
bed and breakfast
castle
cathedral
cinema
department store
exhibition
mosque
museum
palace
stadium
temple
theatre
theme park

Suggestions
What shall we do?
Why don't we visit Windsor Castle?
Shall we go to the cinema?
How about taking a boat trip?
Let's go shopping.
That's a nice idea.
I'd rather go shopping.
I don't mind.
I think that's a good idea.
That's fine with me.
I don't really want to do that.
All right then.

School
cafeteria
classmate
normal
ordinary
packed lunch
secondary school

Uses of *get*
(to) get dressed
(to) get home
(to) get into
(to) get off
(to) get on
(to) get out of
(to) get ready
(to) get to
(to) get up

Study skills 2
Thinking about learning

Are these descriptions true for you? Think about them carefully, then write T (true), F (false) or ? (I'm not sure) for each sentence. You've got three minutes.

1 I'm quite shy. I hate speaking in class.
2 I always worry before a test.
3 I don't feel embarrassed when I make a mistake.
4 I feel stupid when the teacher corrects me.
5 It's helpful if I work with a partner.
6 I like learning new words.
7 I don't understand English grammar. It's too difficult.
8 If I don't write something down, I don't remember it.

Work with a friend and compare your answers. Can you make any suggestions to help your friend?

I don't understand English grammar.

Why don't you look at the grammar notes?

How's it going?

• Your rating

Look again at pages 44 and 45. For each section decide on your rating: Good ✓✓✓ Not bad ✓✓ I can't remember much ✓

• Vocabulary

Choose five words from the Vocabulary list and write them down. Then work with a friend and, for each word, ask: *What does ... mean? How do you spell it?*

• Test a friend

Look again at Units 3 and 4. Think of at least two questions, then ask a friend.

Which shape did you choose in the personality quiz?

What's life like for students in Japan?

• Correcting mistakes

Can you correct these mistakes? In some sentences, there is more than one mistake.

1 ~~Alex is the most nice person of the class.~~
2 ~~Megan is taller her friends.~~
3 ~~I think it is the more beautiful place in our country.~~
4 ~~How about to visit Brighton the next weekend?~~
5 ~~She can't come. She hasn't got too much money.~~

• Your Workbook

Complete the Learning Diaries for Units 3 and 4.

Coursework 2 My guidebook

Read Ana's guidebook, then make your own page about interesting places in your country. Explain how you can get to them from your home.

Getting around

There are a lot of wonderful places to visit in the UK. These are three of my favourites.

The castle at Tintagel

The little village of Tintagel is on the north coast of Cornwall, in southwest England. Its castle is one of the most famous castles in Britain. People say that it was the home of King Arthur in the fifth century and that the ghost of his helper, Merlin the Wizard, visits the cave under the castle.

From London, you can get to Cornwall by train or by coach. I went by coach. It takes quite a long time but it's much cheaper than the train.

Hyde Park

Hyde Park covers 140 hectares and is London's biggest park. It's a popular place for riding and running. People play rugby, football and Frisbee there too. You can go on a boat on the Serpentine, or go swimming at the Lido, or you can just sit in a deckchair and chat to your friends. I particularly like Speakers' Corner – where people stand up and talk about all sorts of different subjects.

I usually get the bus when I go to Hyde Park. If you live in the city centre, you can get a 'travel card', or you can buy tickets at a newsagent's, or you can get them from the machine at the bus stop.

Brighton

Brighton is a fantastic place to go for the weekend. It's on the south coast, not far from London. I love looking round the shops and there are a lot of good cafés and restaurants. If you like old buildings, you can visit the beautiful Royal Pavilion. I like walking along the sea front and going on Brighton pier.

It's easy to get to Brighton from London. You can get the train from Victoria Station or London Bridge Station. It only takes an hour.

Module 3

The future

In Module 3 Steps 1 and 2 you study

Grammar
- Present continuous used for the future
- The future with *going to*
- The future with *will/won't*
- *will* in offers
- First conditional
- *might*
- *will/won't + probably*

Vocabulary
- Names of sports clothes
- At the table

Expressions
- Shopping
- Polite requests

so that you can
- Talk about arrangements and intentions
- Talk about the future and make offers and promises
- Make a conversation in a shop
- Talk about results
- Make a conversation in a restaurant
- Talk about things that are probable and things that aren't certain in the future

Life and culture

The history of the Olympics
Journey into space

Coursework 3

Part 3 Shopping in London
You write about shopping in your town or your capital city.

My favourite clothes shop is Topshop. You can find one in most big towns. I go to the one at Oxford Circus, in the middle of London.
Oxford St

In Step 3 you ...

read
- An interview
- An article about inventions

study
- Adjective/verb + preposition
- Compound nouns
- Skimming
- Identifying the topic

so that you can
- Interview a friend and then write about him/her
- Make predictions about the future

What's it about?

What can you say about the pictures?

Now match the pictures with sentences 1–5.

1 I'll get this blue tracksuit.
2 I'm going to enter the European Junior Championship next year.
3 Could you pass the bread, Ana?
4 If you speak to him, you might think he's human.
5 You might feel homesick.

a

b

c

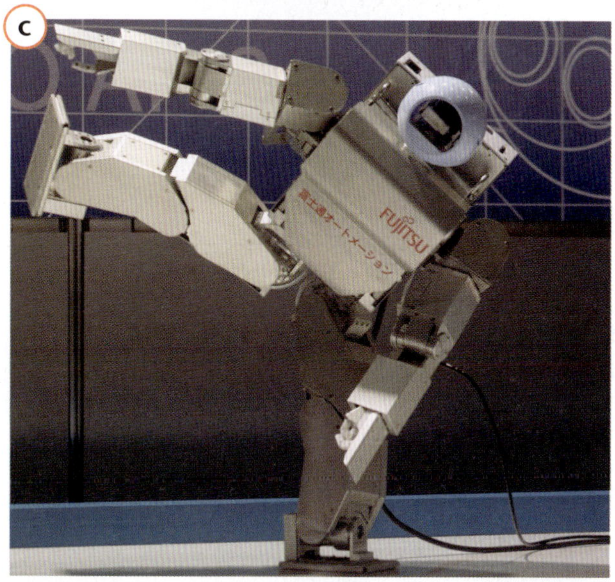

d

e

5 Goals

STEP 1

In Step 1 you study
- present continuous used for the future
- the future with *going to*

so that you can
- talk about arrangements and intentions

1 Share your ideas

a What can you say about the photo? What do you know about sport in the USA?

> A lot of people play American football.

b Look at Len's diary. What can you say about next weekend?

> There's a match on Saturday. They're going to Kansas City.

23 FRIDAY
9.00 Team meeting Room 41
3.30 Training

24 SATURDAY
8.30 Coach; college car park
9.45 Flight AMA 417
10.30 Arrive Kansas City
11.15 Practice
12.00 Lunch
1.30 RAIDERS v ZEBRAS

Meeting notes for Friday
- arrangements for Saturday
- talk about last game
- watch Zebras video

TO DO
Buy present for Kim
Mend motorbike

2 Presentation *Len's diary*

a Read what Len says at the team meeting. Complete the sentences with information from his diary.

Len Murray is a football coach at his local college in Minneapolis. He and his team – the Raiders – often travel long distances to play their matches. It's nine o'clock on Friday morning and Len's talking to the Raiders.

"OK guys, let's begin. First, I'm going to tell you about tomorrow. Then we're going to talk about our last [1]........... . After that, we're going to watch a [2]........... of the Zebras.

So here are the arrangements for tomorrow. As you know, we're playing against the Zebras in [3]........... . Kick-off is at 1.30. We're meeting in the [4]........... and we're leaving at [5]........... . We're getting the plane at [6]........... . There's a practice session at 11.15, then we're having [7]........... at the stadium. Any questions? OK? Well, I've got an important question for you guys: What's going to happen on Saturday?"

> We're going to win!

Listen to Len and check.

b Ask and answer the questions.

1 What are Len and his team going to talk about next?
2 What are they going to do after that?
3 Where are the Raiders playing on Saturday?
4 Who are they playing against?
5 What time are they leaving the college?
6 How are they getting to the airport?
7 Are they having their lunch on the plane?
8 Look again at Len's diary. What's he going to buy? What else is he going to do?

3 Key grammar
The future with the present continuous and going to

Read the examples and complete the explanations. How do you say the example sentences in your language?

We**'re leaving** the college at 8.30 tomorrow.
The Raiders **are playing** against the Zebras next Saturday.

We use the .... for a definite arrangement for the future.

The Raiders **are going to watch** a video.
Len**'s going to buy** a present for his girlfriend.

We use .... + verb to talk about our intentions.

G 6, 7

4 Practice

a Write sentences describing future arrangements. Use the present continous form of these verbs:

go out with	not play	meet	arrive	babysit
not have	come	go		

1 Jay's busy tonight. He's babysitting at the house next door.

1 Jay's busy tonight. He / at the house next door.
2 It's Tamsin's birthday on Friday but she / party.
3 I must go. I / my sister at the school gate.
4 My pen friend / next week. He / at the airport at 2.30 on Tuesday.
5 Martin / Lizzie this evening. They / to the cinema.
6 The Raiders / on the 4th. They've got a free weekend.

b **Test a friend** Write another sentence about an arrangement, but leave a blank. Can your friend guess what's happening?

I'm ..... Pablo after school.

You're meeting Pablo after school.

c What are these people going to do? Ask and answer.

What's he going to do?

He's going to buy a watch.

he / watch

she / room

they / cards

he / bike

she / car

5 Listening and speaking
That's a long way!

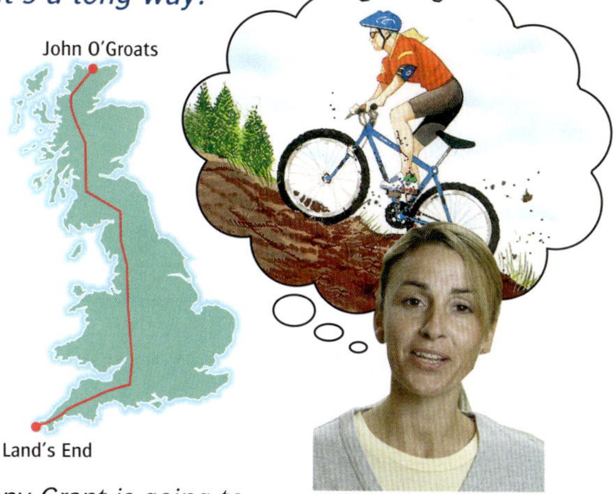

Penny Grant is going to cycle from Land's End to John O'Groats. She wants to raise money for the charity Oxfam.

a Penny's talking about her trip to some students at her son's school. Listen to the first part of her talk. How far is it from Land's End to John O'Groats?

b Read the students' questions. Then listen to the conversation and put the questions in the order you hear them.

4...

1 What's Oxfam going to use the money for?
2 How long is it going to take?
3 How much money are you going to raise?
4 When are you leaving?
5 Where are you going to stay?

c Listen and check. Then work in pairs and imagine one of you is Penny. Ask and answer the questions in 5b.

6 Writing and speaking *Making plans*

Use what you know

Imagine you're going to raise money for a charity. Work with a friend and decide what you're going to do. Write at least three sentences about your plans, then tell the class.

We're going to cycle from Barcelona to Milan. We're leaving next month, on the 12th.

We're going to run / walk / swim ... .

STEP 2

In Step 2 you study

- names of sports clothes
- the future with *will* and *going to*
- *will* in offers
- expressions we use when we're shopping

so that you can

- talk about the future, and make offers
- make a conversation in a shop

1 Key vocabulary *Sports clothes*

Match the words with the pictures. You've got two minutes!

tracksuit swimsuit swimming trunks goggles wetsuit boots socks shorts

1

2

3
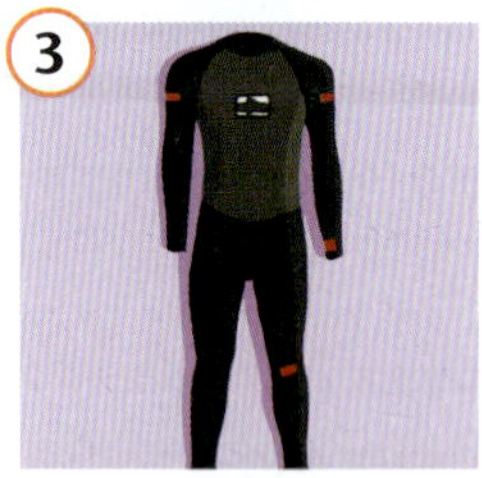

4

5

6

7

8

Listen and check.

Try this!
What other things can you buy at a sports shop? Make a list.

2 Presentation *Of course I will*

a Close your book and listen to the conversation. What colour tracksuit is Ana going to buy?

Ana's in town with Lizzie. They're outside a sports shop.

ANA: I need a tracksuit, Lizzie. I'm going to join a sports club.
LIZZIE: Great! Shall we go in and have a look? I'll give you my expert opinion! ...
ANA: I like this one.
LIZZIE: What size do you take?
ANA: Medium, I think. I'll try it on.
LIZZIE: OK. The fitting room's over there. I'll hold your bag for you.

LIZZIE: Hey, you look great, Ana.
ANA: I'd rather have green, I think. Have they got any green ones?
LIZZIE: I'll ask the assistant.
ANA: Thanks.
LIZZIE: Excuse me. Have you got this tracksuit in green?
ASSISTANT: If you can't see it, we haven't got it. Sorry.
ANA: It doesn't matter, Lizzie. I'll get this blue one. It'll be fine. I won't be a minute.
LIZZIE: OK. Hey, I like these trainers. I think I'll try them on.

b Listen again and follow in your book. Then read these sentences. Which sentence is false?

1 Ana wants to do more sport.
2 Lizzie offers to help Ana choose a tracksuit.
3 Ana wants to be sure it's the right size.
4 Lizzie offers to hold Ana's bag.
5 Lizzie offers to ask the shop assistant.
6 The assistant is very helpful.
7 Ana's going to buy the blue one.
8 Lizzie wants to try some trainers on.

c Match the seven true sentences with a sentence from the conversation.

1 Ana wants to do more sport.
She says, 'I'm going to join a sports club.'

3 Key grammar *The future with* will *and* going to

a How do you say these sentences in your language?

> I'**m going to join** a sports club.
> *We use* going to + *verb to talk about plans and intentions. The decision is already made.*
> I think I'**ll try** them on.
> *We use* will + *verb when we decide to do something at the time of speaking.*
> G ➜ 7, 5a, c

b Complete the example and read the explanation.

> I .... hold your bag for you. *We use* I'll + *verb when we offer to do something.*
> G ➜ 5c

4 Practice

a Make sentences with the right form of *going to* or *will*.

1 These trousers look nice. I think I *'ll try* (*try*) them on.
2 'Why .... (*you/sell*) your bike?' – 'Because I need the money.'
3 'Is it difficult?' – 'No, it's easy. Look! I .... (*show*) you.'
4 We .... (*see*) a film tonight. Would you like to come?
5 'Oh no! The bus is leaving!' – 'Never mind. We .... (*walk*).'
6 I need to get more exercise. I .... (*join*) the local gym.

b Complete and practise the four dialogues. Make offers using *I'll* + these words:

carry that for you. do it. answer it. cook the dinner.

1
The phone's ringing.
I'll ...
2
I'm tired.
I'll ...
3
I'll ...
Thank you very much.
4
Can someone clean the board for me, please?
I'll ...

5 Key expressions *Shopping*

Work with a friend. Match 1–5 with a–e and make five dialogues.

1 Can I try this top on?
2 How much is it, please?
3 Do you like the red one?
4 What size do you take?
5 I'm not sure if they're the right size.

a It's ten ninety-nine.
b Small, I think.
c Why don't you try them on?
d Sure. The fitting room's over there.
e Not really. Have you got a blue one?

6 Key pronunciation /aɪ/ /ʊ/ /æ/

Listen and repeat the words. Find the odd one out each time.

1 /aɪ/ like try give size right
2 /ʊ/ boot look foot put good
3 /æ/ bag hat hand play match

7 Writing and speaking *Buying clothes*

Use what you know

Work with a friend. Imagine you're in a sports shop. Write a short conversation. Then act it.

STEP 3

In Step 3 you	so that you can
• read an interview • study adjective/verb + preposition	• interview a friend and then write about him/her

1 Share your ideas *Sport*

Which sports are you interested in? Which sports are you good at? Which ones do you watch on TV?

I like playing basketball.

2 Reading

a Reading skills *Skimming*

Read the text quickly. You've got one minute!

Now answer the questions. Don't look at the text.

1 This text is from ...
  a a diary. b a magazine.
2 Tom Bradshaw is ...
  a a schoolboy. b a professional athlete.
3 He's interested in ...
  a lots of different sports.
  b one sport in particular.
4 In the future he wants to ...
  a be a successful high jumper.
  b get a well-paid job.
5 Choose at least two adjectives to describe Tom's character:
  shy ambitious kind lazy positive forgetful

b Comprehension check

Listen, and read the text again. Then find:

1 two things Tom likes eating.
2 two things he's good at.
3 two things he's bad at.
4 two things that annoy him.
5 something he's scared of.
6 something he does that's irritating.
7 someone he admires.
8 something he worries about.

c Now find the following information.

1 What competition did he recently win?
2 How high did he jump?
3 Why does he want to go to St Mary's College?
4 What competition is he going to enter next year?
5 What's his goal for the future?

High Hopes!

Tom Bradshaw (16) – high jumper

What's your greatest achievement?
I won the English Schools Championship earlier this year. I jumped two metres and five centimetres.

What's your favourite food?
Sausage sandwiches. And I love cooking curry.

Which three words best describe you?
Ambitious, honest and forgetful.

What are you good at?
The high jump, of course, and chess. I really enjoy playing chess with my dad. I usually win so I guess I'm good at it.

What are you bad at?
Getting up early. And I've got a terrible memory. I'm very bad at remembering people's names, birthdays and things like that.

What things annoy you?
People who talk loudly, especially on their mobile phones. And the rain. I hate training in the rain.

What are you afraid of?
Snakes. My brother has got a pet snake and I'm terrified of it. I can't even look at it.

Have you got any irritating habits?
I interrupt people when they're talking. It drives my friends mad!

Who do you admire and why?
Steve Redgrave, because I think he's the greatest sportsman of all time. He was incredibly successful. He won five Olympic gold medals.

What do you worry about?
Competitions. I never sleep well before an important competition.

What are your plans for the future?
I want to go to St Mary's College. It's got a special High Performance Centre for athletics. I'm going to enter the European Junior Championship next year, and after that I hope I'll go to the World Junior Championship. One day I'm going to be the World Champion!

3 Word work *Adjective/verb + preposition*

a Choose the right preposition to complete the questions.

to	at	of	in	about

1 Can you think of three things you're good .... ?
2 What subjects at school are you interested .... ?
3 Is there anything you're afraid .... ?
4 What do you worry .... ?
5 What things are you bad .... ?
6 What sort of music do you listen .... ?

Remember!

After good at, worry about, *etc. we use a noun or a verb +* -ing.
I'm **good at** volleyball.
I'm **good at** cooking.

b **What about you?** Work with a friend and ask and answer at least three of the questions in 3a.

Writing guide
Writing in the 3rd person

- Change pronouns, verbs and possessive adjectives.
  I'm good at ... > He/She's good at ...
  I go ... > He/She goes ...
  My brother ... > His/Her brother ...
- Use adjectives in your description.
  He/She's a very ambitious person.
- Use a noun or verb + *-ing* after:
  interested in, good/bad at, worry about, etc.
  He's bad at remembering people's names.
  like, enjoy, love, hate
  She enjoys watching basketball on TV.

4 Speaking and writing *An interview*

Use what you know

Choose at least three questions from the interview with Tom Bradshaw. Ask a friend and make notes of the answers.

Name: Encar
Question: What are you good at?
Notes: swimming / every weekend

Now write about your friend.

I spoke to Encar. She's good at swimming. She goes swimming every weekend.

Extra exercises

1 Complete the conversation. Choose from a–h.

A: Can I help you?
B: [1] ....
A: What size do you take?
B: [2] ....
A: Here you are, size five.
B: [3] ....
A: I'll get a size four. ...
Here you are.
B: [4] ....
A: They're £45.
B: [5] ....
A: I'll put them in a bag.

a Why don't you buy them?
b These are better. How much are they?
c Yes, can I try these shoes on?
d OK. I'll take them, please.
e Thanks. Oh, they're a bit big.
f Size five, I think.
g I won't be a minute.
h How much is it?

2 Choose the right words and make complete sentences.

1 (*I'll / I'm going to*) learn French next year.
2 Kevin is at the door. (*I'll / I'm going to*) go and open it.
3 (*We'll / We're going to*) give Brett a skateboard for his birthday. We bought it last week.
4 (*Are you going to / Will you*) see a film tonight?
5 These trousers are nice. I think (*I'll / I'm going to*) try them on.
6 Dan and Chris (*will / are going to*) play tennis after school on Friday.

3 Read the conversation and choose the right words for each space.

A: Manchester United [1] .... against Arsenal tomorrow afternoon.
B: I know. Kick-off is at three. [2] .... the game?
A: Yes. Sarah, Matt and I [3] .... at John's house. Do you want to come?
B: Sorry, I can't. Alex and I [4] .... There's a new sports shop in town.
A: Oh, what [5] .... ?
B: I'm not sure. Maybe some new trainers.

1	a are playing	b played	c playing
2	a Are you going to watch	b Do you watch	c Do they watch
3	a meet	b are meeting	c is meeting
4	a go shopping	b are shopping	c are going shopping
5	a are you going to buy	b do you buy	c did you buy

4 Read the text. Put the letters in order and make 'sports clothes' words.

I went to the beach with some friends last weekend. I wore my new [1]*sitiwusm* but John forgot his swimming [2]*sntrku* so he couldn't go in the sea. I took my [3]*egslgog* because my eyes hurt in the sea water. Jeremy and Celine really like surfing. They brought their [4]*siwtesut* and they spent nearly all day in the water. In the afternoon it got colder so I put on my [5]*riatucstk*. It was a great day.

5 Choose the right words.

1 .... go to the party on Friday?
a Are you b Are you going to c Do you
2 I don't think .... on time. The traffic is terrible.
a we'll arrive b we arrive c we're arriving
3 I like this swimsuit. I think .... try it on.
a I'm b I will c I'll
4 Don't worry. This .... hurt.
a isn't b won't c isn't going
5 James really believes .... famous.
a he's going to be b he'll c he's being

6 How do you say these sentences in your language?

1 Have you got any blue ones?
2 That's really irritating.
3 I'm bad at remembering names.
4 I'm not sure if it's the right size.
5 How much is it, please?
6 It drives my friends mad when I interrupt them.

Extra reading

Life and culture

The history of the Olympics

How many Olympic sports can you think of?

The ancient Olympics

Nobody knows exactly when the Olympic Games began, but historians think that the first games were in 776BC. Athletes from all over Greece came to compete in a town called Olympia. There was only one event. It was a running race called the 'stade'. The first Olympic champion was Coroebus of Elis. He was a cook.

The games were very popular. Soon there were more events, for example, wrestling and horse races. All the athletes in the ancient Olympics were men and, when they competed, they wore no clothes. The games took place every four years, for a thousand years. In AD394 the Roman Emperor Theodosius stopped them for religious reasons.

The modern Olympics

In 1887, at the age of 24, the Frenchman Pierre de Coubertin decided he wanted to restart the Olympic Games. It took a long time, but finally the first modern Olympic Games began in Athens in April 1896. Thirteen countries took part. There were nearly 300 competitors in nine different sports.

Pierre de Coubertin also designed the Olympic rings. Each ring represents one of the five continents and the Olympic flag contains at least one colour from every national flag.

Today, the Olympic Games are the world's most famous sports competition. The modern Olympics take place every four years in a different city. In 2004 they were again in Athens. Over 11,000 athletes from 203 countries competed in 28 sports, 3,000 years after the first Olympic Games.

Task

Read the text, then answer the questions.

1 When do historians think that the first Olympics took place?
2 How many different nationalities competed in the first games?
3 Who won the only event?
4 Which events did the organisers of the early games add?
5 Who was Pierre de Coubertin?
6 Where did the first modern Olympics take place?
7 How many athletes were there in 1896?
8 Why are there five rings on the Olympic flag?
9 How many athletes competed in the 2004 Olympics?

When is the next Olympics going to take place? Do you know where?

ABOUT THE ANCIENT GREEKS

Nike was the Greek goddess of victory. The Greeks believed she had wings, and could run and fly at great speed.

6 Choices

STEP 1

In Step 1 you study	so that you can
• vocabulary for 'at the table' • first conditional • polite requests	• talk about results • make a conversation in a restaurant

1 Key vocabulary *At the table*

a Match the words with the things in the picture. You've got one minute!

plate knife fork spoon glass
serviette menu salt and pepper

Listen and check.

b Match these definitions with the words in 1a.

1 You eat spaghetti with it. *fork*
2 You put water in it.
3 You put them on your food.
4 You eat soup with it.
5 You put your food on it.
6 You cut your meat with it.
7 You read it when you choose your meal.
8 You wipe your hands and mouth with it.

c **Test a friend** Tell your friend to close the book. Choose a definition and read it out. Can your friend remember the word?

You eat soup with it.

A spoon.

2 Presentation *You'll be ill if you eat all that*

a Read the menu, then listen to the conversation and follow in your book. How many people are having a starter?

Ana's at a restaurant with the Grant family.

CHARLIE: Let's go over there. If we sit by the window, we'll be able to see the river.

MRS GRANT: OK. ... Has everyone got a menu? What do you fancy?

MR GRANT: I think I'll have pâté, and then I'll have steak with black pepper sauce. Ana, what would you like?

ANA: I'm not sure. What's 'plaice'?

MR GRANT: It's fish. Let's have a look. 'Plaice with mushrooms and tomatoes.' That'll be nice.

ANA: Yes. Could I have that, please? I won't have a starter, thanks.

MR GRANT: OK. What about you, Charlie?

CHARLIE: I'd like pizza, please, and can I have a plate of chips as well? And for dessert I'd like apple tart and ice cream.

MRS GRANT: You'll be ill if you eat all that.

CHARLIE: No, I won't. I'm starving. Could you pass me the bread, Ana?

MR GRANT: What about you, Penny? Are you going to have a starter?

MRS GRANT: Maybe. But if I have a starter, I won't have a dessert. I think I'll try the carrot and orange soup. Then I'll have curry.

MR GRANT: OK. I'll call the waiter. ... Could we order now, please?

WAITER: Certainly. What would you like?

Starters

Melon
Goat's cheese on toast
Carrot and orange soup
Mushroom pâté

Main courses

Steak with black pepper sauce
Plaice with mushrooms and tomatoes
Chicken curry with basmati rice
Vegetable lasagne
Cheese and ham pizza with a green salad

Desserts

Apple tart
Chocolate and coffee mousse
Ice cream

b Are these sentences true or false? Correct the false sentences.

1 The restaurant is by the river.
2 Mr Grant's a vegetarian.
3 He isn't going to have a starter.
4 Ana wants fish.
5 She's going to have a starter as well.
6 Charlie wants a main course, a dessert and some chips too.
7 Mrs Grant doesn't think he'll be able to eat all that.
8 Charlie's very hungry.
9 Mrs Grant's going to have a dessert.

3 Key grammar *First conditional*

Read the examples and complete the explanation.

If I **have** a starter, I **won't have** a dessert.
You'**ll be** ill if you **eat** all that.
We use If + ... *simple, and* will *or* won't *+ verb to describe the result of a possible future action.*

G 8

Remember!

The future of can *is* will/won't be able to.
If we sit here, we'**ll be able to** see the river.
Charlie **won't be able to** eat all that.

G 5e

4 Practice

Put the verbs in the right form and write complete sentences.

1 Penny and Tim will be annoyed if Charlie's late.

1 Penny and Tim .... (*be*) annoyed if Charlie .... (*be*) late.
2 If you .... (*ask*) Jay, he .... (*give*) you Ana's address.
3 You .... (*not be*) healthy if you .... (*not eat*) enough fruit.
4 If we .... (*visit*) Lightning Ridge, we .... (*be able to*) watch the famous goat races.
5 If I .... (*not do*) my homework now, I .... (*not be able to*) go out later.
6 Charlie .... (*eat*) your chips if you .... (*not finish*) them.

5 Key expressions *Polite requests*

a Match 1–6 with a–f and make six sentences.

1 Could you	a have some water, please?
2 I'd like plaice	b ice cream, please?
3 Could I have a	c we order now?
4 Could I	d pass me the salt, please?
5 Could	e serviette?
6 Can I have some	f and chips, please.

b If you have time, make different sentences with the words in 1–6.

6 Key pronunciation /e/ /eɪ/ /ʌ/

Listen and repeat the words. Find the odd one out each time.

1 /e/ bread egg plaice friend head
2 /eɪ/ main steak plate said plaice
3 /ʌ/ onion come curry lunch goat

7 Speaking *At a restaurant*

Use what you know

Work in groups. Imagine it's a special occasion and you're having a meal together at a restaurant. One person is the waiter. Choose what you want from the menu in 2a, then tell the waiter. If you prefer, invent your own menu.

STEP 2

In Step 2 you study
- the future with *will* and *might*
- *will/won't + probably*

so that you can
- make promises
- talk about things that are probable and things that aren't certain in the future

1 Share your ideas

What can you say about the photo? Imagine you're going to Africa. What do you think life will be like there?

> I'll see some fantastic animals.

2 Presentation

You might not enjoy it!

a Listen to Lizzie and her parents and follow in your book. How do they all feel?

Lizzie wants to go to Kenya next summer, to a camp for students.

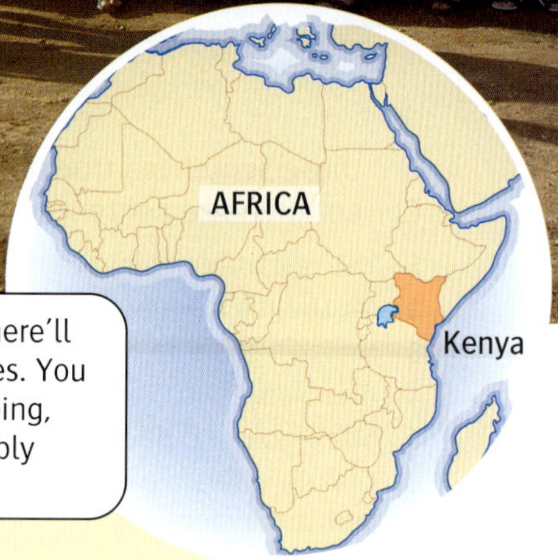

It'll be very hot, Lizzie. There'll be hundreds of mosquitoes. You won't be able to go clubbing, you know. And you probably won't like the food.

Your dad's right, Lizzie. You might feel homesick. You never know. You might not enjoy it. And you might be ill. You might catch malaria! And what about Martin?

Don't worry, Mum! I'll take my malaria tablets every day, I promise. And if I feel homesick, I'll ring you. I'll send you lots of letters and emails. I promise I won't forget! Martin says he'll write to me every week. I'll probably miss him a bit, I suppose. But I'm sure I'll be fine.

b Match questions 1–9 with answers a–i.

1. Will it be very hot in Kenya?
2. Will there be many mosquitoes?
3. Will Lizzie be able to go clubbing?
4. Will she like the food?
5. Will she feel homesick?
6. Is Lizzie's mum sure she'll be ill?
7. What will Lizzie take every day?
8. What other promises does she make?
9. Will Martin forget about Lizzie?

a. No, she isn't, but it's possible.
b. No. He'll write to her every week.
c. She might like it. She might not like it.
d. No, she won't.
e. Yes, it will.
f. She might miss her family. She can't be sure.
g. She'll contact her parents regularly.
h. Yes, there will.
i. Some special tablets.

Listen and check, then ask and answer the questions.

3 Key grammar will *and* might

a How do you say these sentences in your language?

I'**ll** send you lots of emails.
I promise I **won't** forget.

We use will *and* won't *to make promises.*

G 5c

b Complete the explanations.

It'**ll** be very hot in Kenya.
You **probably won't** like the food.

We use .... *or* .... *+ verb when we are sure about something in the future.*

We use probably *with* .... *or* .... *if we aren't completely sure.*

Lizzie **might** be ill. They don't know.
She **might not** like it.

We use .... *or* .... *+ verb when we don't know what will happen.*

G 5b, d, 10

4 Practice

a Imagine other promises that Lizzie makes. Use *I'll* or *I won't* + one of these verbs.

wear	go out with	send
be	go	forget

1 Don't worry! I *won't go* to any dangerous places.
2 I promise I .... careful.
3 Martin, I .... anyone else!
4 I .... a hat if it's very hot.
5 I .... you a postcard, I promise.
6 I .... to take my malaria tablets.

Try this!
What will Lizzie be able to do in Kenya? Write four sentences with *She'll be able to ...*

SWXM XN THX XNDXXN XCXXN
STXDY WXLD XNXMXLS
LXXRN XNXTHXR LXNGUXGX
GX XN SXFXRX

b Make sentences using *'ll/will probably* or *probably won't* + the verb in brackets.

1 How about asking Martin? He *'ll probably help* (*help*) us.
2 This sauce isn't very nice. You .... (*like*) it.
3 The Grants .... (*have*) a holiday abroad. They haven't got enough money.
4 Tom's a brilliant high jumper. He .... (*win*) an Olympic medal one day.
5 If Lizzie goes to university, she .... (*study*) zoology.

c Lizzie's dad is always pessimistic! Make dialogues using *might/might not* + these words.

bite us	crash	like it	rain	pass

1 I think my exam went quite well.
– You never know. You *might not pass.*
2 Why don't you try this carrot and orange soup?
– No, thanks. I ....
3 What a lovely dog! Look! – Be careful! It ....
4 Why are you taking an umbrella? It's sunny!
– You never know. It ....
5 How about going by plane? – You're joking! It ....

d **What about you?** Talk about your future.

I probably won't live here for the rest of my life. I might go abroad.

5 Listening *Song*

a Close your book and listen. Who is 'you' in the song?

b Listen again. What does the singer say about the future? What promises does he make?

Tomorrow I'll miss you.

6 Writing and speaking *Going abroad*

Use what you know

Imagine you're going to spend a month abroad. What will it be like? What are your worries? What and who will you miss? Write your ideas, then tell a friend.

I'm going to spend a month in Brazil. I think it'll be really interesting. I might feel homesick. I'll probably miss my dog.

STEP 3

In Step 3 you
- read an article about artificial intelligence
- study compound nouns

so that you can
- make predictions about the future

1 Share your ideas *Science fiction?*

What do you think artificial intelligence is? Do you watch science fiction films? Which films have got robots in them?

I don't watch a lot of science fiction films, but I think the *Star Wars* films had robots in them.

Artificial intelligence

by KEVIN ANDERSON

1 Predicting the future isn't easy. In 1943 Thomas Watson, chairman of the company IBM, said, 'I think there's a world market for about five computers.' Even in the 1970s, many experts were saying, 'No one will want a computer in their home.' But today, computer technology is everywhere.

2 'You already have several computers in your kitchen,' says Dr Rodney Brooks of MIT (the Massachusetts Institute of Technology), pointing to the computer chips in our coffee makers, fridges, washing machines and ovens. It's almost impossible to imagine a world without computers.

3 Dr Brooks is director of MIT's Computer Science and Artificial Intelligence Laboratory. He says that computers are not only becoming more common, they're getting smarter too. They're starting to think.

4 Scientists at AI Research are developing their own thinking robot, called Hal. Child expert Anat Treister-Goren is teaching Hal to speak. She talks to him and reads him children's stories. Baby Hal is growing up fast, and his language level is improving quickly. Soon, if you speak to him, you might think he's human!

5 AI experts are optimistic. They hope that, one day, intelligent machines will be all around us. Perhaps everyone will have a Hal – their own personal assistant. If you've got a question, Hal will know the answer. If you want to go on a trip, Hal will be able to make all the arrangements. He'll never get tired, he'll never be ill and he'll never get angry. The technology is almost here. Think about it. Would you like your own 'Hal'?

2 Reading

a Read the newspaper article. Who or what is Hal?

b **Comprehension check**
Listen, and read the text again. Answer the questions.

1 Was Thomas Watson optimistic about the future of computers?
2 In the 1970s, were the experts' predictions right?
3 Where are the computers in a kitchen?
4 Computers are changing. How?
5 Why is Hal special – what is he learning to do?
6 Who is his teacher and what does she do?
7 How do we know that Hal is a good learner?
8 Will Hal be like a human being?

c **Reading skills** *Identifying the topic*
Read the text again. Think about the topic of each paragraph then match the five paragraphs with these headings.

Paragraph 1 d

a Now they can think!
b Hal's future.
c Computers in the home.
d The experts were wrong.
e Hal's education.

3 Word work *Compound nouns*

a Match a word on the left with a word on the right and make ten compound nouns. You might need your dictionary for some of them.

1 coffee maker

1	coffee	jam
2	dining	park
3	traffic	room
4	car	machine
5	bus	clock
6	mobile	stop
7	alarm	star
8	washing	chip
9	computer	phone
10	pop	maker

b If you have time, think of some more compound nouns.

post office

Writing guide *Expressing your ideas*

You can use these words when you write about what you think.

- Giving an opinion
  In my opinion, … I think …
  I don't think …
- Showing that you aren't sure
  The climate might/might not …
- Describing consequences
  If people don't change, … will …
- Expressing hope
  I hope I'll …
  I hope there won't be …

4 Speaking and writing
My future predictions

Use what you know

What will life be like in the future? What sort of things will we be able to do? What are your hopes? What are your worries about the future? Talk about your ideas, then write at least three predictions.

I don't think money will exist in the future.
I hope I'll be able to find an interesting job.
A lot of wild animals might disappear.

Extra exercises

1 Complete the conversations.

1 I'm singing at the concert on Friday. Can you come?
  a Yes, I won't be there.
  b Yes, I'll be there.
  c Yes, you will.
2 Will you have a holiday this year?
  a Yes, I'm going.
  b I probably will.
  c Yes, I did.
3 Is Peter going to come to the cinema with us?
  a He's going.
  b He'll go.
  c He might come.
4 What will you buy Sarah for her birthday?
  a I buy a coffee maker.
  b I'll probably buy a coffee maker.
  c She'll buy a coffee maker.
5 Can you please buy some milk at the shops?
  a I promise I won't.
  b I might not forget.
  c OK, I won't forget.

2 Choose the right words.

1 If you .... hard, you'll fail your exam.
  a 'll work
  b don't work
  c couldn't work
2 If we go home now, we .... see the beginning of the film on TV.
  a 'll be able to
  b be able to
  c can be
3 I'll be in my office if you .... anything.
  a will need
  b need
  c would need
4 We .... a video this evening if there are some good films in the shop.
  a 'll get
  b get
  c won't get
5 You .... there on time if you don't leave immediately.
  a won't get
  b don't get
  c couldn't get

3 Put the words in the right order and make sentences.

1 Liam will probably want to watch the film on TV.

1 watch / probably / Liam / on / to / want / TV / film / will / the
2 might / year / I / study / next / French
3 'll / shopping / go / probably / on / we / Saturday
4 finish / be / homework / will / you / to / your / able / ?
5 won't / I / out / probably / go / tonight
6 they / to / might / party / come / our / not

4 Put the letters in the right order and make seven words for things we use at the table. Then use the words to complete the text.

EATLP EKINF UEMN PONSO KROF
EITSEVTER EPRPEP

My parents decided to try a new restaurant last weekend, so I went with them. The evening started well and the [1].......... looked good. I had soup for my starter but the waiter didn't bring a [2].......... so it was getting a bit cold before I could eat it. Then, for my main course, I had steak and a huge [3].......... of chips, but my [4].......... wasn't very good and I couldn't cut the steak. I didn't like the sauce. There was too much [5].......... in it. I didn't have a [6].......... and I dropped some sauce on my trousers. For my dessert I had apple tart but I didn't have a [7].......... or a spoon so I ate it with my fingers!

5 Complete the conversation. Use your imagination.

A: What would you like to have for your starter?
B: Can I have .... ?
A: And for your main course?
B: Could .... ?
A: Would you like anything to drink?
B: Yes, I'd ....
A: Anything else?
B: ....

6 How do you say these sentences in your language?

1 What do you fancy?
2 Let's go clubbing.
3 I promise I won't forget.
4 I'm starving.
5 I think I'll try the pâté.
6 I'll miss you.

Extra reading

Life and culture

Journey into space

How many planets can you name? What can you say about them?

Where would you like to go for your next holiday? If you like the sun, perhaps you might choose to go to the beach. Or maybe you'd prefer to go skiing in the mountains? Or how about a holiday in space?

You probably think you'll never be able to go on holiday in space, but in fact space tourism is already here – if you're extremely rich! If you want to go into space today, it will be very expensive. An eight-day trip to the International Space Station costs about $20 million.

Fifty years ago, only the richest people could travel by plane, but now 1.6 billion people fly every year. So perhaps the same thing will happen with space travel. The USA, Britain, France, Germany, Japan, Russia and India are all planning to build 'space planes'. So, in the future, space travel might be a lot cheaper and easier.

The Japanese company Shimizu Space Systems is already building a space hotel. It will have 64 rooms, each with a fantastic view! As well as enjoying the view, you will be able to go for a spacewalk, or have fun in a zero-gravity play room. So start to save your money now, if one day you want to have your birthday, or even your wedding, in space.

ABOUT SPACE

Astronauts in the International Space Station sneeze about 100 times a day. In space, dust never stops moving.

Task

Are these sentences true or false? Correct the false sentences.

1. At the moment, tourists can't go into space.
2. Space tourism is very expensive.
3. Only astronauts can stay at the International Space Station.
4. Fifty years ago, no one travelled by plane.
5. Many countries are building 'space planes' at the moment.
6. Perhaps space travel will become cheaper in the future.
7. There is already a hotel in space.
8. If you go to the Japanese space hotel, you won't be able to go outside.

Module 3 Review

Grammar check

1 The future with the present continuous, *going to* and *will*

Work it out for yourself

A Look at the examples and answer the questions.

1 • *Present continuous*

Alice is looking at her calendar.

ALICE: ***I'm meeting** Paul at 10.30 next Saturday.*

Is Alice talking about
a) a possibility, or
b) an arrangement?

2 • *going to*

Alice knows that she needs some new swimming goggles for Saturday.

ALICE: ***I'm going to buy** some new goggles.*

Is Alice talking about
a) an intention, or b) a possible future action?

3 • *will*

Alice is phoning Paul about next Saturday.

ALICE: *There's a bus at ten o'clock.*

PAUL: *The bus takes fifteen minutes. So **you'll be** at the beach at 10.15.*

Is Paul talking about a) a simple future fact, or b) an intention?

ALICE: *Can you meet me at the bus stop?*

PAUL: *Sure. **I'll meet you** there at 10.15.*

Does Paul decide to meet Alice at the bus stop a) when they're talking on the phone, or b) before their conversation?

B Match verb forms a–c with explanations 1–4.

a *will* b *going to* c *the present continuous*

1 .... – a new decision that we make at the time of speaking; sometimes it's an offer or a promise.

2 .... – a definite arrangement for the future; something that is already organised.

3 .... – an intention for the future; a decision that we make before the time of speaking.

4 .... – a simple fact about the future; we're sure about it.

Check that you can

1.1 • understand the difference between the three future forms.

Choose the right answer.

1 I won't be here next week. (*I'll start / I'm starting*) my holiday on Monday.
2 I want to try surfing. (*I'll / I'm going to*) buy a surfboard and a wetsuit.
3 Can you open this box for me? – Yes, (*I'm going to / I'll*) use a knife.
4 We can get the 8.30 bus. So (*we're going to / we'll*) be in town at 9.00.
5 My dad's free tomorrow. (*He isn't working / He won't work*).
6 I like this top. I think (*I'll try / I'm trying*) it on.
7 Where's my mobile? I feel really ill. (*I'm phoning / I'm going to phone*) the doctor.

1.2 • use the three future forms.

Complete the conversations. Use *will, going to* or the present continuous.

1 A: Shall I buy this CD for Alice?
B: No, she .... (*not like*) it. She hates Robbie Williams.

2 A: Have The Raiders got a match on Saturday?
B: Yes. They .... (*play*) against The Giants.

3 A: Do you want to come to the cinema?
B: I'm not sure, but I .... (*phone*) you later.

4 A: Why are you making a list?
B: Because I .... (*do*) the shopping.

5 A: Will you write to me?
B: Yes, I promise I .... (*write*) to you every day.

2 The first conditional
Work it out for yourself

A **Look at the pictures. Steve wants to go to Sarah's party tonight, but he also wants to see the basketball final.**

STEVE: *If I **go** to Sarah's party, I**'ll have** a good time. But if I **go** to the party, I **won't see** the final.*

Match explanations 1 and 2 with a and b.

1 The result of a possible future action.
2 A possible future action.

a he won't see the final.
b If he goes to Sarah's party,

B **Answer the questions and complete the explanation.**

1 What tense do we use to describe a possible future action?
2 What tense do we use to describe the result of this action?

In first conditional sentences, we use .... in the *if* clause, then .... or .... + verb.

Check that you can

- **use the first conditional.**

Write sentences. Start with *If* ... .

1 If Kate goes to America, I'll miss her.

1 It's possible Kate will go to America. I'll miss her.
2 It's possible I'll be late. Will you wait for me?
3 Why don't you wear your boots? Then your feet won't get wet.
4 I think I'll do my homework now. Then I'll be able to go out later.
5 It's possible my brother won't get a ticket. Then he won't be able to go to the match.
6 You must put salt in the soup or it won't be nice.

3 *will, might* and *probably*
Work it out for yourself

Six runners are at the start of a race. They're all thinking about the race. How optimistic are they? Put the names in order from 1 to 6. Number 1 is the most optimistic runner.

JAMES: I might not win.
JACK: I'll probably win.
MARK: I won't win.
PETE: I probably won't win.
TOM: I'll win.
DAVE: I might win.

Check that you can

3.1 • **use *might* and *might not*.**

Rewrite the sentences in a different way, without changing the meaning.

1 I might be a famous scientist one day.

1 Perhaps I'll be a famous scientist one day.
2 Perhaps I'll discover the secrets of the universe.
3 Perhaps I won't pass my exams.
4 Perhaps my dreams won't come true.
5 Perhaps I won't be successful.

3.2 • **use *probably* with *will* and *won't*.**

Rewrite the sentences in a different way, without changing the meaning.

1 I'll probably go shopping at the weekend.

1 I think I'll go shopping at the weekend.
2 I'm almost sure I won't buy anything.
3 I don't think England will beat Brazil tonight.
4 But I think it'll be an exciting match.
5 I don't think I'll go out this evening.
6 I think I'll stay at home.

Vocabulary and expressions

Sports clothes
boots
goggles
shorts
socks
swimming trunks
swimsuit
tracksuit
wetsuit

Shopping
fitting room
(to) have a look
(to) try on
I'm not sure if they're the right size.
What size do you take?
Medium, I think.
Can I try this top on, please?
Do you like the red one?
Have you got a blue one?
How much is it?

Competitive sport
achievement
(to) admire
ambitious
(to) enter a competition
goal
high jump / high jumper
medal
performance
successful
well-paid

Adjective/verb + preposition
afraid of
bad at
good at
interested in
listen to
worry about

At the table
dessert
fork
glass
knife
main course
menu
(to) order
pepper
plate
salt
serviette
spoon
starter

Polite requests
Can I have some ice cream, please?
Could I have a serviette?
Could you pass me the salt, please?
I'd like plaice and chips, please.

Artificial intelligence
computer chip
(to) develop
expert (n.)
(to) imagine
(to) improve
laboratory
(to) predict
prediction
robot

Compound nouns
alarm clock
bus stop
car park
dining room
mobile phone
pop star
traffic jam
washing machine

Study skills 3
Making a vocabulary notebook

If you make your own vocabulary notebook, this is a good way to help you to remember new words. You can record vocabulary in lots of different ways, for example:

1 Have a double page for each letter of the alphabet. Write the words with their translation.
2 It's often useful to record the part of speech too. Some words can be a noun or a verb: *to walk (v.), a walk (n.).*
3 Underline the part of the word that is stressed, for example, *<u>am</u>bulance.*
4 Make lists of words for different topics, for example:
Sports and activities *swimming*
Sports equipment *goggles*
5 You might like to include a section for words with the same form but different meanings: *to work (= 1 to do a job) to work (= 2 to function).*

Which of these ways do you think is the most useful?

How's it going?

• Your rating
Look again at pages 66 and 67. For each section decide on your rating: Good ✓✓✓ Not bad ✓✓ I can't remember much ✓

• Vocabulary
Write six words from the Vocabulary list. For each word, (1) write its translation, (2) write the part of speech (noun, verb, etc.) and (3) if there is more than one syllable, underline the stressed syllable.

• Test a friend
Look again at Units 5 and 6. Think of at least two questions, then ask a friend.

Why did Ana want to buy a tracksuit?

What was the name of the song in Unit 6?

• Correcting mistakes
Can you correct these mistakes? In some sentences there is more than one mistake.

1 ~~I go shopping tomorrow. I'll buy some swimming trunks.~~
2 ~~We will going to leave at nine thirty.~~
3 ~~I will free the next week.~~
4 ~~If Charlie will be late, Penny will be annoyed.~~
5 ~~I can come tomorrow. I'm not sure.~~

• Your Workbook
Complete the Learning Diaries for Units 5 and 6.

Coursework 3 My guidebook

Read Ana's guidebook about shopping in London, then make your own page about interesting shops and markets in your town, or in your capital city.

Shopping in London

London is a fantastic place for shopping. These are some of my favourite shops.

There are many different markets in London and they're all busy and colourful. Camden Market is a good place for clothes, jewellery and souvenirs.

My favourite clothes shop is Topshop. You can find one in most big towns. I go to the one at Oxford Circus, in the middle of London.

Selfridges, in Oxford Street, is one of the biggest department stores in London. Many famous stars visit it when they're in the UK. It has got six floors and you can buy nearly everything there. It has got a hairdresser, an optician, a travel agent and 11 cafés and restaurants too.

If you like reading horror stories, go to Forbidden Planet in New Oxford Street. It's a bookshop with a big variety of science fiction, fantasy, horror and comics.

Davenports Joke Shop is an amazing place. It's over a hundred years old. It sells all sorts of jokes and puzzles. You'll find it at Charing Cross underground station.

The Virgin Megastore at Piccadilly Circus is one of the biggest and best music shops in the UK. If you're looking for a rare record, you'll probably find it there. It's open from 9.00 in the morning until midnight from Monday to Saturday, and from 11.30 to 6.00 on Sunday.

Module 4

Your world

In Module 4 Steps 1 and 2 you study

Grammar
- Present perfect: affirmative, negative and questions
- Present perfect + past simple
- Present perfect + *ever* and *never*
- Present perfect + *just*
- Present perfect + *for* and *since*
- *How long ...?*

Vocabulary
- Using a machine
- Names of outdoor activities

Expressions
- *I think so. / I don't think so.*
- Time expressions with *for* and *since*

so that you can
- Describe achievements and changes
- Say what people have done and when they did it
- Talk about using a machine
- Talk about experiences
- Describe things that happened a short time ago
- Talk about present situations and how long they have continued

In Step 3 you ...

read
- A newsletter about a campaign
- A biography

study
- The infinitive of purpose
- Prepositions of time
- Understanding the main idea
- Guessing meaning from context

so that you can
- Write a letter about a campaign
- Write a biography of a singer or band

Life and culture

Saving Gwrych Castle
Poem

Coursework 4

Part 4 Useful information
You write some useful information for a visitor to your country.

Have you ever been to the UK? If you haven't, y this information helpful.

Postcards and letters
When you go to the post office to buy your stamps, you can say:

I want to send a postcard to Cairo, please.

How much is a stamp for Egypt?

It's easy to see letter boxes in the UK, because they're usually red.

Shopping
The shops usually open at 9.00 or 9.30 and close about 5.30. Supermarkets

What's it about?

What can you say about the pictures?

Now match the pictures with sentences 1–5.

1 Have you plugged it in?
2 She started a campaign to save the rainforest.
3 Modern medicine has saved the lives of millions of people.
4 I've just driven a racing car.
5 We've been here for hours!

a

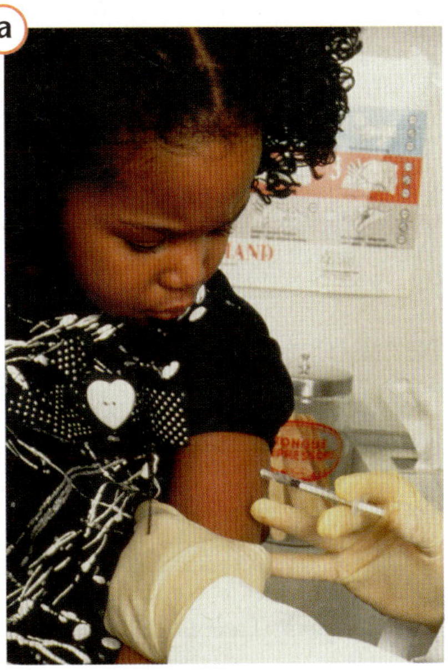

b

c

d

e

7 Achievements

STEP 1

In Step 1 you study	so that you can
• present perfect: affirmative, negative and questions	• describe achievements and changes

1 Share your ideas

What can you say about the photos? What positive things can you see? What negative things can you see?

We can communicate with people all over the world.

A lot of people haven't got enough to eat.

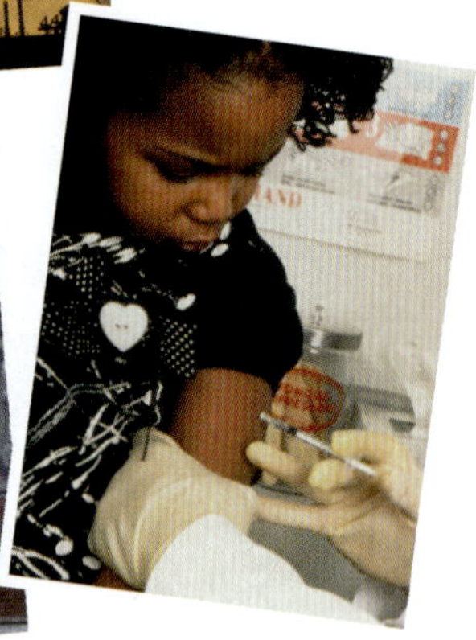

2 Presentation *I've changed the world!*

a Read the conversation between the brain and the Earth. Are they both sure that the world is better now?

I've changed the world!

Yes, the world is very different now. But have you forgotten about me?

No, I haven't. People can visit every corner of the Earth now. I've produced the car and the aeroplane.

Yes, you've made some amazing machines.

And I've built some fantastic cities.

Yes, but you've polluted the air and the oceans, and you've destroyed thousands of animals and plants. ¹.......... You haven't taken care of the environment.

You're right. ².......... Modern medicine has saved the lives of millions of people.

Yes, I know. ³.......... Your technology hasn't produced enough food for everyone.

Perhaps not. ⁴.......... I've invented the telephone and the computer. I've put satellites into space.

Yes, you've improved communications. But people haven't learnt to share. ⁵..........

That's true. But I've done some incredible things.

And you've made a lot of mistakes too.

b Complete the conversation with these sentences.

- a They're often selfish and unkind.
- b But people everywhere can communicate easily.
- c The natural world is in danger.
- d But a lot of people are starving.
- e But people are much healthier now.

Listen to the complete conversation and check your answers.

3 Key grammar *Present perfect*

a Complete the questions and answers, then complete the explanation. Use the right form of *have*.

Our cars I/We/You/They Modern life He/She	have 've has 's	polluted the planet.
I/We/You/They He/She	haven't hasn't	learnt to share.

.... Has	you he	forgotten?	Yes, I have . / No, I .... Yes, he .... / No, he hasn't.

We form the present perfect using have/.......... , ... / hasn't + *the past participle of the verb.*
We use it to describe the present result of a past action.
We often use it to talk about changes and achievements.

G ▸ 11a-b

See Irregular Verbs, page 143.

b Look at 2a again. Find at least ten past participles and complete the lists.

Verb	*build*	*change*
Past participle	*built*	*changed*

4 Practice

a Make questions, then work with a friend and ask and answer.

> Have people travelled to the Moon?

> Yes, they have.

1 to / people / have / Moon / travelled / the ?
2 walked / Mars / on / people / have ?
3 the / has / changed / climate ?
4 we / environment / the / have / protected ?
5 pollution / trees / has / a lot of / destroyed ?
6 stayed / the / has / same / world / the ?

b Make sentences in the present perfect affirmative or negative, using these past participles.

done lost stopped arrived built put made changed

1 My watch *has stopped* . It needs a new battery.
2 I can't find my mobile. I think I .... it.
3 This isn't right. He .... a mistake.
4 I can't go to bed. I .... my homework.
5 Martin and Lizzie are here but Jay ....
6 Look! They .... a little house in the tree.
7 Helen .... the colour of her hair. She looks completely different.
8 You .... the butter in the fridge. Look! It's melting.

5 Listening and speaking
What a difference!

a [CD] Listen to the radio advert, then answer these questions.

1 Who do you think will buy the *TeenTamer* CD-ROM?
2 Think of adjectives to describe Eddie before and after his parents bought *TeenTamer.*

b [CD] Read the sentences, then listen again. Which two things aren't mentioned in the advert?

1 Eddie has tidied his room.
2 He's done the shopping.
3 He's washed the car.
4 He hasn't watched too much TV.
5 He hasn't argued with his parents.
6 He hasn't come home late.
7 He's bought some flowers for his mother.
8 He's finished his homework.
9 Now he's going to do the washing up.

c Imagine you're the perfect teenager! Tell the class about things you have or haven't done this week.

> I've cooked the supper. I haven't shouted at my sister.

6 Writing and speaking
Another advert

Use what you know

Work with two friends. Write an advert for a CD-ROM called *ParentTamer.* Then act your advertisement.

ParentTamer has changed my life. Look! My dad has tidied my room.

STEP 2

In Step 2 you study
- vocabulary for using a machine
- present perfect and past simple
- *I think so. / I don't think so.*

so that you can
- say what people have done and when they did it
- talk about using a machine

1 Key vocabulary *Using a machine*

Put the actions in the right order. What do you do first? Then what do you do? You've got one minute!

1 plug in c

a

turn on

b

turn off

c

plug in

d

unplug

e

put in

f

take out

Listen to the actions in the right order and check your answers.

2 Key pronunciation /ɪ/ /ɒ/ /aʊ/

Listen and repeat. Practise the vowel sounds and the links between the words.

1 /ɪ/ plug‿**it**‿**in** put‿**it**‿**in**
2 /ɒ/ turn‿it‿**on** turn‿it‿**off**
3 /aʊ/ take‿it‿**out**

3 Presentation *Have you plugged it in?*

a Close your book and listen to the conversation. What has Mr Grant forgotten to do?

Tim Grant has got a new DVD player but he isn't sure how it works.

CHARLIE: Hi, Dad. What's that?
MR GRANT: I've bought a DVD player. It was really cheap.
CHARLIE: Great! When did you buy it?
MR GRANT: I bought it yesterday, at the market.
CHARLIE: Is it OK?
MR GRANT: Yes, I think so, but I'm not sure how it works.
CHARLIE: Have you looked at the instructions?
MR GRANT: Yes, I have. I looked at them last night with Penny. She said, 'Charlie'll know!'
CHARLIE: Have you connected it to the TV?
MR GRANT: Yes, I've done that. Look!
CHARLIE: Er ... have you plugged it in?
MR GRANT: Of course I have!
CHARLIE: And you've put a DVD in. Mmm ... that's strange. Have you forgotten anything?
MR GRANT: No, I don't think so.
ANA: Wait a minute! You haven't turned the TV on!
MR GRANT: Oh no! How stupid of me!

b Listen again and follow in your book, then answer these questions.

1 What has Mr Grant bought?
2 When did he buy it?
3 Was it expensive?
4 Has he looked at the instructions?
5 When did he look at them?
6 What three things has Mr Grant done?
7 What hasn't he done?

4 Key grammar *Present perfect and past simple*

Look at the examples and complete the explanations.

I've **bought** a DVD player.
I **bought** it yesterday.
I **bought** it at the market.

Mr Grant **has looked** at the instructions.
He **looked** at them last night.

We use the ..... to connect the past with the present. We don't say when the action happened.
*We use the ..... if we say when something happened in the past (*yesterday*) or if we give more details (*at the market*).*

G 12

5 Practice

a Match sentences 1–5 with sentences a–e.

1 I've broken my leg.
2 I broke my leg last Christmas.
3 The coffee maker doesn't work.
4 Ana broke the lamp in her room yesterday.
5 I'm sorry. I've broken your sunglasses.

a Charlie mended it when he came home from school.
b I can't do any sport.
c I'll buy you another pair.
d I spent three days in hospital.
e Has someone broken it?

b Choose the right words and make complete sentences.

1 I started school when I was four.

1 (*I've started / I started*) school when I was four.
2 We can go out now. Look! The rain (*stopped / has stopped*).
3 An Englishman (*invented / has invented*) the World Wide Web in 1991.
4 They aren't ready. They (*didn't finish / haven't finished*) their breakfast.
5 Where's my bike? Someone (*took / has taken*) it!
6 What's the matter? (*Have you lost / Did you lose*) something?
7 (*I bought / I've bought*) a tracksuit at the market last Saturday.
8 (*I've done / I did*) my homework. (*I've done / I did*) it before dinner.

Try this!

Match the two halves of each word and find eight past participles.

CHANG TEN BRO PED TAK GED TID GHT
STOP IED KEN BOU ED PLUG EN FORGOT

c What about you? Talk about your favourite books and films. Work with a friend and make another conversation like this one:

A: What's your favourite book?
B: *Northern Lights*. Have you read it?
A: Yes, I have. I read it last term.

6 Key expressions

I think so. / I don't think so.

Put the sentences in the right order. Then practise the conversation with a friend.

– No, I don't think so. They might be in the box somewhere.
– I don't understand how this works.
– Yes, I think so. But I can't find them.
– Are there any instructions with it?
– Did you leave them in the shop?

7 Writing and speaking

How does it work?

Use what you know

Imagine you've got, for example, a new computer game or a video player. You aren't sure how it works. Work with a friend and write a conversation.

A: Hi. I've got a problem! I've bought a new ...
B: Wow! When did you buy that?
A: I bought it ... . Anyway, I'm not sure how it works.
B: Well, have you ...?

Practise your conversation.

STEP 3

In Step 3 you
- read a newsletter about a campaign
- study the infinitive of purpose

so that you can
- write a letter about a campaign

1 Share your ideas *Our endangered planet*

How many endangered animals can you think of? Why is our environment in danger? What are some of the problems?

We're polluting oceans and rivers.

endangered /ɪn'deɪŋdʒəd/ adj
endangered animals/birds/plants animals and plants that are now rare and that might soon disappear *The Siberian tiger is one of the most endangered animals in the world.*

2 Reading

a Read the text. What campaign did Janine Licare start? Why?

Take Action!

Issue 27

If you care about the environment, you'll really enjoy this month's newsletter. Let's go to Costa Rica and see how one determined teenager has tried to change the world.

Janine Licare was only nine years old when she decided to *take action*. She was worried because the rainforest around her home in Manuel Antonio, Costa Rica, was disappearing. The animals and birds were disappearing too. So, together with a friend, Janine started a campaign to protect her local environment. They called it *Kids Saving the Rainforest*.

Janine Licare at her research centre

The aims of KSTR are to teach children about the rainforest and to help the animals that live there, especially the endangered Mono Titi monkey.

Janine has achieved a lot. She has

Mono Titi monkey, Costa Rica

- raised more than $50,000
- planted over 4,800 trees
- found over 250 volunteers to work with her
- helped many injured birds and animals
- started a variety of different projects, such as 'Adopt-a-tree'
- worked with other schoolchildren around the world
- developed an environmental library and research centre.

Janine in the forest near her home

Janine has appeared in several magazines, and she has been on the National Geographic TV channel as well. She has also developed a special website: www.kidssavingtherainforest.org Why don't you have a look?

'It is very important that we save the rainforest. If the rainforest disappears, then so will our planet.' Janine Licare

b Comprehension check

Listen, and read the text again. For each sentence write T (true), F (false) or ? (the text doesn't say).

1 Manuel Antonio is a place in Costa Rica.
2 The rainforest near Janine's home has disappeared.
3 Janine started KSTR on her own.
4 Her campaign has been very successful.
5 She has paid over 250 people to help her.
6 The research centre is open every day.
7 Janine has become quite famous.
8 The KSTR website is very popular.

c Reading skills
Understanding the main idea

1 What is the topic of the text?
  a famous kids
  b a successful campaign
  c Costa Rica

2 What do you think is the main idea of the text? Read the beginning and the end again, then choose the best answer.

It's about ...
  a a young girl's campaign to protect the rainforest.
  b the importance of protecting trees.
  c young people helping animals.

3 Word work *The infinitive of purpose*

We use *to* + verb when we talk about the purpose of something.

Their aim is **to help** animals.
They started a campaign **to protect** the environment.

The 'infinitive of purpose' often answers the question *Why?*
Why did they start a campaign? – To protect the environment.

Match 1–6 with a–f and make complete sentences.

1d Lizzie will need a hat to wear in the sun.

1 Lizzie will need a hat	a to study English.
2 We've raised enough money	b to see Janine Licare.
3 Ana's come to London	c to save water.
4 Janine appeared on TV	d to wear in the sun.
5 I've started a campaign	e to talk about her campaign.
6 They visited Costa Rica	f to build a new library.

Writing guide *Writing a letter*

- **Address and date**
  Put your address (with the postcode) in the top right-hand corner, and add the date below.
- **Begin your letter:**
  Dear + the name of the person/group you're writing to.
- **Explain why you're writing.**
  I'm writing to tell you about ...
  My friends and I have started a campaign to ...
- **Think of a good way to finish.**
  Would you like to write about our campaign in your newsletter?
- **Endings**
  You can use:
  With best wishes from ...
  Best wishes, ... + your name
  Yours sincerely, ...
  Yours sincerely is more formal than *Best wishes.*

71 Lincoln Road
Derby
DB12 9RS
10th February

Dear Take Action!
I'm writing to tell you about our new campaign to

4 Writing *A letter*

Use what you know

Imagine you've started a campaign, for example, to protect your local environment. Write a letter to *Take Action!*

What's the aim of your campaign?
My friends and I have started a campaign to plant trees / to clean our neighbourhood / to protect an old building / to recycle rubbish.

Think of a name for your campaign. When did you start it?
Our campaign is called 'Trees please!' We started it six months ago.

What have you done?
We've achieved a lot. For example, we've written an article for our local newspaper.

Extra exercises

1 Complete the conversations. Use *one* word.

1 A: Has Nick come home?
B: I think .... , but I haven't seen him.
2 A: What time is it?
B: I don't know. My watch has ....
3 A: I've hurt my leg.
B: When .... you do it?
4 A: Has Sally had her dinner?
B: I don't .... so. I'll ask her.
5 A: I don't know how it ....
B: Have you read the instructions?

2 Complete the text with these words.

plugged it in   put in   turned it off   unplugged   turned on   took out   turned off   turned it on

I was watching a film on DVD last night when I noticed a strange noise and I thought it was the disc. I 1.......... the DVD and I 2.......... the DVD player. I couldn't see a problem so I 3.......... a different disc and 4.......... the DVD player again, but the strange noise came back. Then I decided it was the TV so I 5.......... and 6.......... it at the wall. After a few minutes I 7.......... again and 8.......... , and everything was OK. Isn't technology amazing!

3 Complete the conversations.

1 When did you take your driving test?
a I've taken it.
b I took it yesterday.
c Yes, I did.

2 What's the matter? What's happened?
a I've hurt my knee.
b Liz has an accident.
c Someone takes our car.

3 Have you finished your homework?
a No, I haven't.
b No, I've got it.
c No, I didn't.

4 Have you bought any milk?
a No, I didn't.
b No, I haven't.
c No, I won't.

5 Have you had a good day?
a Yes, we did.
b Yes, we do.
c Yes, we have.

4 Complete the conversation. Choose from a–h.

A: Hello, Lisa. What's the matter?
B: 1..........
A: No, I haven't. Have you looked in all your pockets?
B: 2..........
A: Have you used it today?
B: 3..........
A: Were you at home?
B: 4..........
A: Well, did you put the phone in your bag?
B: 5..........
A: Look! There it is, under the desk.

a No, I've used it today.
b Yes, I have. I think I've lost it. Mum will be angry.
c Yes, I've been in my bedroom.
d I can't find my mobile phone. Have you seen it?
e Yes, I was in my bedroom.
f I think so, but I'm not sure.
g Yes, I think I lost it. Mum will be angry.
h No, but I used it last night.

5 Complete the questions. Then write the answers. Use the present perfect.

1 *Has Kevin done the washing up?*
No, he hasn't done the washing up. He's done the shopping.

1 Kevin / do / the washing up? (*the shopping*)
2 they / build / a new gym? (*a new swimming pool*)
3 Sam / buy / a coat? (*a shirt*)
4 Julie / argue with / her parents? (*her best friend*)
5 they / learn / Spanish? (*Italian*)
6 you / do / Exercise 6? (*Exercise 5*)

6 How do you say these sentences in your language?

1 Has he read the instructions? – Yes, I think so.
2 I don't think so.
3 I'm not sure how it works.
4 How stupid of me!
5 We haven't taken care of the environment.
6 You've changed. You look completely different.

Extra reading

Life and culture

Saving Gwrych Castle

Are there any famous old buildings in your town? What do you know about them?

My name is Mark Baker and I was seven years old when I first saw Gwrych Castle. I was in the car with my parents when we drove past it. I fell in love with the place immediately.

It looks very old, but it's quite modern. A rich man called Lloyd Bamford-Hesketh built the castle in 1819. He liked medieval castles so he decided he wanted one!

Gwrych Castle in Wales

In the last hundred years, the castle has been many different things, from a restaurant to the location for a Hollywood film. However, nobody has lived there for a long time. When I saw it, I felt sad because it's in very poor condition. Some of the walls have fallen down, and the glass from the windows has gone. When it rains, everything gets wet.

I decided I wanted to do something to protect the castle so, when I was 11, I started a campaign to save it. Later, this became the Gwrych Castle Preservation Trust.

We have done a lot to help the castle. We have held different events to raise money, and I have given lots of talks about the castle and its history. I have written three books about the castle and I have even met the Prince of Wales and the Prime Minister! You can see our website at http://www.gwrychtrust.co.uk.

I hope that we will be able to save the castle, so that people from all over the world will be able to come here and enjoy it.

ABOUT CASTLES

There are over 400 castles in Wales. In fact, it is often called 'the land of castles'. The most famous one is Caernarfon Castle.

Task

Read the text and these sentences. For each sentence, write T (true), F (false) or ? (the text doesn't say). Correct the false sentences.

1. Mark Baker is seven years old.
2. Gwrych Castle is over two hundred years old.
3. It is one of the oldest castles in Wales.
4. At the moment it is a hotel.
5. The castle has fallen down.
6. The Prime Minister has visited the castle.
7. The castle is famous all over the world.
8. Mark Baker lives there.
9. He wants to save the castle.
10. You can read about Gwrych Castle on the Internet.

8 Experiences

STEP 1

In Step 1 you study
- names of outdoor activities
- present perfect + *ever* and *never*
- present perfect + *just*

so that you can
- talk about experiences
- describe things that happened a short time ago

1 Key vocabulary *Outdoor activities*

a Match the words with the photos.

climbing sailing canoeing snowboarding
skateboarding surfing bungee-jumping scuba-diving

Listen and check.

b Can you think of any other outdoor activities? You've got one minute!

Try this!

Find eight activities and make three lists: indoor activities, outdoor activities, both.

LINGBOW LFGO HINGFIS ETICSATHL
BLETA NISTEN MINGSWIM
NNINGRU KERSNOO

2 Presentation *I've never done that!*

a Listen to the advert and follow in your book. Which activity would you like to try?

b Match questions 1–5 with answers a–e.

1 Has the *Titanic* sunk to the bottom of the sea?
2 Have you ever been to the edge of space?
3 Has Oscar ever tried zorbing?
4 Has Emily ever driven a racing car?
5 Has she tried zorbing?

a Yes, she has.
b No, she hasn't.
c No, never!
d Yes, it has.
e Yes, he has.

Now ask and answer the questions.

Extraorc

http://www.extraordinaryexperiences.com

extraordinaryexperiences.com
Try something NEW!

You've read about the *Titanic*. Perhaps you've seen the film. But you've never seen the real ship – until now! We'll take you to the bottom of the Atlantic and you'll see the real *Titanic*!

More info

Have you ever been in a Mig 25? Have you ever travelled at 2,800 kph? Have you ever been to the edge of space – 25 kilometres above the Earth? No? Then why not try it?

More info

3 Key grammar
Present perfect + ever *and* never

Read the examples and the explanations. How do you say the examples in your language?

> I've done a bungee-jump.
>
> *We use the present perfect to talk about our experiences in general. We don't say when they happened.*
>
> Has he **ever** travelled in space?
>
> *We often use* ever *in questions about past experiences, when we mean 'until now'.*
>
> Emily has **never** tried zorbing.
>
> Never *means 'not ever'. We use it with the affirmative form of the present perfect.*
>
> G ▶ 11c, f

4 Practice

a **What about you?** Make true sentences using *I've ... or I've never ...* .

1 I've never tried zorbing.

1 try / zorbing
2 go / to England
3 climb / a mountain
4 go / sailing
5 do / a bungee-jump
6 ride / a horse
7 go / skateboarding
8 swim / in a river

b Now work with a friend. Ask and answer at least three questions about the activities in 4a.

Have you ever been to England?

No, I haven't.

Now meet two of our customers:

'I've just tried zorbing. It's amazing! A zorb is an enormous plastic ball. You get inside it and go down a hill at 60 kph!'
Oscar Wood, New York

More info

'I've been scuba-diving. I've done a bungee-jump. I've swum with dolphins. And I've just driven a Formula 1 racing car. But I've never tried zorbing!'
Emily Smith, New York

More info

5 Key grammar *Present perfect* + just

Read the example and the explanation. How do you say the example in your language?

> I've **just** driven a racing car.
>
> *We use the present perfect +* just *for something that happened a short time ago.*
>
> G ▶ 11d

6 Practice

Work with a friend. Ask and answer.

What have they just done?

1

get off / plane

2

do / washing up

3

arrive / station

4

drop / eggs

7 Writing and speaking *My experiences*

Use what you know

Write at least two
- things you've done. *I've been to lots of theme parks.*
- things you've never done, but would like to do. *I've never done a bungee-jump. I'd like to try it one day.*
- questions with *ever*. *Have you ever fallen asleep in the cinema?*

Now talk about your experiences, and ask and answer your questions.

STEP 2

In Step 2 you study
- present perfect + *for* and *since*
- *How long ...?* + time expressions

so that you can
- talk about present situations and how long they have continued

1 Share your ideas

Have you ever been to London?
What do you know about it?
Where are Ana and Charlie?

The river in London is called the Thames.

2 Presentation

We've been here for hours!

a Close your book and listen to the conversation. Is Ana going to meet Jay in Hyde Park this evening?

Ana's on the London Eye with Charlie. Their pod has stopped at the top.

CHARLIE: Why aren't we moving? I'm getting bored. We've been here for hours!
ANA: No, we haven't. We've been here for five minutes – since quarter past three. I looked at my watch when we stopped.
CHARLIE: That's your mobile. I bet it's Jay.
ANA: Oh shut up, Charlie!
... Hi, Jay! I'm on the London Eye with Charlie. It's fantastic.
JAY: Great. Er, listen. I haven't seen you for ages. Er, are you doing anything this evening?
ANA: No, I don't think so. Oh, we've started to move again.
JAY: OK. Well, I'll ring you later.
CHARLIE: How long have you known Jay?
ANA: Since I arrived in London. I met him in Hyde Park.
CHARLIE: Is he your boyfriend?
ANA: No, he isn't.
CHARLIE: Well, he's just phoned you.
ANA: And I've just said he isn't my boyfriend!

b Listen again and follow in your book. Are these sentences true or false? Correct the false sentences.

1 At the beginning of the conversation, it's twenty past three.
2 Ana and Charlie aren't moving.
3 They've been at the top for a very long time.
4 Jay saw Ana yesterday.
5 Ana was talking on the phone when they started to move again.
6 Ana has known Jay since they were children.
7 Ana has just telephoned Jay.

3 Key grammar *Present perfect +* for *and* since

Complete the examples with *for* or *since*. Which tense do you use here in your language?

How long have they been at the top?

NOW

It stopped at 3.15.

They've been there .... five minutes.
They've been there .... 3.15.

We use for *and* since *to answer the question* How long ...?
We use the present perfect + for *to show a period of time.*
We use the present perfect + since *to say when the period of time started.*

G ▶ 11e

4 Practice

a Complete the sentences. Use the right form of the verb, and *for* or *since*. For each sentence, use the same verb twice.

like	work	live	be	know	play

1 The Grants live in London. They've lived there for twenty years.

1 The Grants / in London. They /there .... twenty years.
2 My sister / married to a football coach. They / married .... December.
3 Jay / Martin .... ages. He / him very well.
4 Ana / the piano. She / it .... she was four.
5 Sue / in a language school .... 1998. She / with students from all over the world.
6 Lizzie really / listening to modern jazz. She / it .... a long time.

b **What about you?** Make questions with *How long* + verbs from 4a, then ask and answer.

How long have you known Daniel?

I've known him for three years.

c Talk about your things. Change the underlined words.

A: I like your <u>bag</u>. How long have you had it?
B: I've had it <u>for ages</u>.
A: Where did you get it?
B: <u>It was a birthday present from my aunt</u>.

5 Key expressions *Time expressions with* for *and* since

a Put the time expressions in the right list.

for	*since*
ages	*I arrived in London*

a long time   Christmas   a few weeks
several years   last term   hours
five minutes   a couple of days
the day before yesterday
quarter past three   the Friday before last
the nineteenth century

b **Test a friend** Think of a sentence with *for* or *since*, then write it with a blank.

We've had our dog ..... eight years now.

Can your friend complete the sentence?

6 Key pronunciation *Stress in words*

a Listen and say these words.

1 ● worked lived
2 ● • driven travelled
3 • ● produced improved
4 • ● • forgotten polluted

b Now listen to some more words and repeat. Which group do they belong to? Which is the odd one out?

7 Listening and speaking *My favourite people*

a Listen to Mike talking about three of his favourite people. Match the descriptions with the photos. Who are Lily, George and Vlad?

A Lily

B George

C Vlad

Lily is Mike's .....

b Listen again, then ask and answer these questions.

1 How long has George known Mike?
2 How long has George lived in the same house?
3 Has Mike known Lily for a long time?
4 Where did he meet her?
5 How many times have they been out together?
6 When was the last time Mike saw Lily?
7 When did Mike start writing to Vlad?
8 How many times has Vlad visited Mike?
9 Has Mike written to him recently?

Listen and check.

8 Writing and speaking *Who is it?*

Use what you know

Write a description of someone you know using *for* and *since*.

She's 82 years old. She's lived in her house for sixty years. She's been married to my great-grandfather since she was seventeen.

Read your description to a friend. Can your friend guess who it is?

STEP 3

In Step 3 you
- read a biography
- study prepositions of time

so that you can
- write a biography of a singer or band

1 Share your ideas *Music*

What kind of music do you like?
Have you ever been to a concert?

I've never been to a big concert.

2 Reading

a Read the text. Find at least two facts that you didn't know about U2.

U2 The World's Biggest Band

I still haven't found what I'm looking for

I have climbed the highest mountains
I have run through the fields
Only to be with you
Only to be with you

I have run, I have crawled
I have scaled these city walls
These city walls
Only to be with you

But I still haven't found
What I'm looking for

In 1978 four friends at a high school in Dublin won a local music competition. Eighteen months later, in September 1979, they released their first record. It was a big hit. Today, the Irish rock band U2 are one of the most successful 'supergroups' of all time. Thanks to songs like *With or without you* and *I still haven't found what I'm looking for*, they are famous all over the world.

They have sold more than 100 million albums worldwide. They have performed in front of millions of people and their live concerts are always a huge success. They have won numerous music awards, including 14 Grammy* awards. They have also written songs for several Hollywood films, for example, *Batman Forever*, *Goldeneye* and *Mission Impossible 2*.

Their lead singer is Paul Hewson, known as Bono. *Q* magazine has called him 'the most powerful man in music'. Bono has used his fame to campaign for international human rights and to fight AIDS in Africa.

* A Grammy is an American award for the best recorded music.

■ 24

b Reading skills

Guessing meaning from context

Find these words in the text. Read what comes before and after. What part of speech are the words? What do you think they mean?

released hit album performed
huge award fame

'Released' is a verb.
I think it means ...

c Comprehension check

Listen, and read the text again. Then answer the questions.

1 How did U2 begin their music career?
2 When did they have their first hit?
3 How long have they been famous?
4 Where do they come from?
5 How many albums have they sold?
6 Are their concerts usually popular?
7 Can you hear their music at the cinema?
8 What is Bono's real name?
9 What sort of campaigns has he supported?

3 Word work *Prepositions of time*

a Complete the sentences, using the right preposition.

in at on

Tina has been a fan of U2 for many years. She went to her first U2 concert [1]......... 1992. It was [2]......... the spring, [3]......... Easter, but she bought her ticket [4]......... December. The concert was [5]......... 15th April. She's never forgotten the date. [6]......... Saturday, 15th April, she met her hero, Bono. The concert finished [7]......... 10.45. After the concert, she waited outside the theatre. Finally, [8]......... one o'clock [9]......... the morning, the band left the theatre and she got Bono's autograph.

b Complete the rules using *in*, *at* or *on* and find an example each time.

seasons: *winter*
festivals: *Easter*

1 We use .... with clock times and the names of festivals.
2 We use .... with parts of the day, and with months, years and seasons.
3 We use .... with days and dates.

Writing guide *Writing a biography*

- Decide which singer or band you want to write about. Make a list of everything you know.
  personal details, type of music, most famous songs, etc.
- Organise the information in chronological order.
  They started to play together in ... . Then they ...
- Use prepositions of time.
  They had their first hit in ...
- Give details of their albums, their concerts, their awards and other achievements.
  They've had five number one hits.
- Finally, write about you. Describe how long you've been a fan, your favourite records, etc.

4 Writing *A biography*

Use what you know

Write a short biography of your favourite band or singer. Explain why you like them.

Where do they come from?
What kind of music do they play?
How many albums have they made?
Have they won any famous awards?
How long have you been a fan?
Have you ever been to one of their concerts?

Read your biography to a friend.

Extra exercises

1 Choose the right words.

1 I haven't seen him since ....
a a few weeks b a long time c last week

2 Jane has been ill for ....
a half past one b a couple of days
c the day before yesterday

3 We've known the Jacksons since ....
a a long time b last Christmas c a few weeks

4 That song has been number one since ....
a two months b several weeks c March

5 You haven't called me for ....
a ages b last week c the Tuesday before last

2 Put the words in the right order and make sentences.

1 been / you / rock / ever / to / have / a / concert ?
2 table / Gillian / played / has / tennis / never
3 just / car / Thomas / new / a / bought / has
4 never / riding / been / I / 've
5 have / machine / had / you / long / your / how / washing ?
6 come / just / Switzerland / we / in / back / holiday / from / 've / our

3 Complete the conversations.

1 Have you ever won an award?
a No, I didn't.
b Yes, I did.
c No, never!

2 *Spiderman* is on TV tonight. Do you want to see it?
a No thanks, I saw it.
b No thanks, I've seen it.
c No, I haven't.

3 Where's Fiona?
a She was leaving.
b She's just left.
c She's never been.

4 How long have you lived here?
a For ages.
b We lived here for two years.
c I haven't.

5 Have Lisa and Tony been married for a long time?
a Yes, they are.
b Yes, they have.
c Yes, they were.

4 Read the text and choose the right word for each space.

I went to the USA last summer on an activity holiday. It was great! We stayed near a huge lake so we went [1] .... every day, and we sometimes went [2] .... on the river, too. One weekend we travelled to the mountains and we went [3] .... – that was exciting. It was quite hot and there wasn't any snow, so we didn't go [4] .... On the last day of our holiday we all went to the river and we went [5] .... – we jumped from a bridge over the river. That was scary, but I enjoyed it.

1	a bowling	b sailing	c running
2	a climbing	b canoeing	c snowboarding
3	a climbing	b surfing	c scuba-diving
4	a running	b sailing	c snowboarding
5	a fishing	b surfing	c bungee-jumping

5 Complete the conversation. Use your imagination.

A: Have you ever .... ?
B: No, I haven't. Have you?
A: Yes, ...
B: Oh, really. When?
A: ....
B: What was it like?
A: It was ....

6 How do you say these sentences in your language?

1 I haven't seen you for ages.
2 Oh, I've just cut my hand!
3 How long has Sam known Mark?
4 I'm getting bored.
5 Why not try it?
6 That's the phone. I bet it's Susan.

Extra reading

Life and culture

Poem

Look at the picture. What do you think this poem is about?

What has happened to Lulu?

What has happened to Lulu, mother?
What has happened to Lu?
There's nothing in her bed but an old rag-doll
And by its side a shoe.

Why is her window wide, mother,
The curtain flapping free,
And only a circle on the dusty shelf
Where her money-box used to be?

Why do you turn your head, mother,
And why do tear drops fall?
And why do you crumple that note on the fire
And say it is nothing at all?

I woke to voices late last night,
I heard an engine roar.
Why do you tell me the things I heard
Were a dream and nothing more?

I heard somebody cry, mother,
In anger or in pain,
But now I ask you why, mother,
You say it was a gust of rain.

Why do you wander about as though
You don't know what to do?
What has happened to Lulu, mother?
What has happened to Lu?

Charles Causley

ABOUT CHARLES CAUSLEY

Charles Causley was one of the UK's best loved poets. He wrote poetry for children and for adults. He was born in 1917 in Cornwall in southwest England and he lived there most of his life. He died on 4th November 2003, aged 86.

Task

Read the poem, then look at the questions and share your ideas.

1 Who do you think is speaking in the poem?
2 What do you think has happened? Where has Lulu gone?
3 What has she taken with her?
4 What did she write before she left?

Module 4 Review

Grammar check

1 Present perfect
Work it out for yourself

A Look at the two pictures of Frank Miller and answer the questions.

YESTERDAY TODAY

1 Which picture does the sentence describe?
Frank ***has cut*** *his hair and he****'s bought*** *some new clothes.*

2 Can you think of another sentence in the present perfect to describe picture B? Use the verb *change*.

B Choose the right explanation.

The present perfect describes …

a a past action.
b the present result of a past action.
c something that is happening now.

Check that you can

- **use the present perfect.**

Write complete sentences for 1–6, using the verbs in brackets. Then match 1–6 with a–f.

1 *I've forgotten your address. c*

1 I (*forget*) your address.
2 Someone (*take*) my book.
3 I (*not finish*) my dinner.
4 (*you/see*) my keys?
5 My watch (*stop*).
6 Pete (*break*) his leg.

a I can't find them.
b It isn't in my bag.
c Is it 15, Mill Road?
d What time is it?
e I'll be ready in five minutes.
f He's in hospital.

2 Present perfect and past simple
Work it out for yourself

A Match Pictures A and B with sentences 1 and 2.

Helen's at the bus stop.

Joe's at school.

1 ***I missed*** *my bus*. (past simple)
2 ***I've missed*** *my bus*. (present perfect)

B Match 1 and 2 with a and b. Then complete the explanations with *past simple* or *present perfect*.

1 Joe has arrived. a He was late.
2 Joe arrived at 9.20. b Look, he's over there.

We use the .... to connect the past with the present. We don't say when the action happened.

We use the .... to talk about a past action. We often say when it happened and give more details.

Check that you can

- **understand the difference between the present perfect and the past simple.**

Choose the right answer.

1 Jack (*arrived / has arrived*). He's in the living room.
2 Look at the colour of the water! Something (*polluted / has polluted*) the river.
3 Scientists (*have invented / invented*) the digital camera in 1991.
4 We (*saw / 've seen*) the new Johnny Depp film last night.
5 Why isn't my mobile working? – I don't know. I (*haven't touched / didn't touch*) it.
6 (*Did you finish / Have you finished*) the washing up? Shall we play cards now?

3 Present perfect + *ever/never*

Work it out for yourself

A **Look at the time line and complete the sentence.**

5 YEARS AGO A YEAR AGO TODAY

——— ever/never ———→

Dean Williams is an Olympic athlete. What are Dean's experiences up to today?

He .... (win) a silver medal and a bronze medal.

B **Now complete these sentences. Use *ever* and *never*.**

Has Dean .... (win) a gold medal?
– No, he .... (win) a gold medal.

Check that you can

3.1 • **use the present perfect for experiences.**

Make sentences about Dean's other experiences. Use the present perfect with the verbs in the box.

travel	make	write	meet

1 He's written a book.

1 There's a book in the library by Dean.
2 There's a photo of Dean with the Queen.
3 In his passport there are visas for China and Japan.
4 There's a video in the shops called *Training with Dean*.

3.2 • **ask people about their experiences.**

Make questions with *Have/Has* + *ever*. Then ask and answer the questions.

1 Have you ever seen a ghost?

1 you / see / a ghost?
2 you / win / a competition?
3 your school / be / on TV?
4 you / write / a poem?

4 Present perfect + *just*

Work it out for yourself

Choose a or b.

*Polly **has just** painted the door.*

Polly painted the door ...
a a long time ago.
b a short time ago.

Does *just* mean a or b?

Check that you can

• **describe things that happened a short time ago.**

Make two true sentences. Use the present perfect + *just*.

I've just opened my book.

5 Present perfect + *for/since*

Work it out for yourself

A **Read the example and complete the explanation with *present perfect* or *present simple*.**

—— FOR an hour ——→
SINCE 2.15

At 3.15 someone at the station asked Harry:
*How long **have you been** here?*

We use the .... when we talk about a period of time up to the present.

B **Read the explanations and answer the question.**

We use the present perfect with *for* to describe a period of time.
We use the present perfect with *since* to say when the period of time started.
What is Harry's answer to the question in A?
Give two possible answers: *I've been here ... .*

Check that you can

• **ask questions with *How long?* and answer them with *for* or *since*.**

Ask each person a question and give two answers.

Seth, how long have you ...?
– I've had it for ... . I've had it since ... .

1 Seth bought his computer two years ago. (*have*)
2 Sally went to live in London when she was six. She's sixteen now and she's still in London. (*live*)

Vocabulary and expressions

Using a machine
instructions
(to) plug in
(to) put in
(to) take out
(to) turn off
(to) turn on
(to) unplug

Expressions
I think so.
I don't think so.

The environment
(to) adopt
campaign
(to) destroy
endangered
ocean
(to) plant
(to) pollute
(to) produce
(to) protect
rainforest
starving
(to) take action
(to) take care of
volunteer

Outdoor activities
bungee-jumping
canoeing
climbing
sailing
scuba-diving
skateboarding
snowboarding
surfing
zorbing

Time expressions with *for* and *since*
a couple of days
a few weeks
a long time
for ages
for hours
several years
the day before yesterday
the Friday before last
the nineteenth century

Music
album
award
biography
fame
hit (n.)
lead singer
live (adj.)
(to) perform
(to) release (a record)
supergroup

Study skills 4 Learning to listen

How can you improve your listening? Read the list and think about each item. In your opinion, is it important or not very important? Give each sentence a rating from 1 to 5. You've got three minutes.

5 = very important   1 = not important

1 The pictures and photos will help you to understand the texts and dialogues.
2 It's important not to panic. Try to relax!
3 You don't need to understand every word.
4 The first time you listen, try to get a general idea of what is happening.
5 Make sure everyone in the class is quiet when you're listening.
6 Tell the teacher if you can't hear.
7 Before you listen, start to think about the situation or the topic.
8 If you close your eyes, it will help you to concentrate.
9 Remember that a lot of students feel nervous when they're listening to a foreign language.

Work with a friend and compare your ratings. Did you have the same opinions?

How's it going?

• Your rating
Look again at pages 88 and 89. For each section decide on your rating: Good ✓✓✓   Not bad ✓✓
I can't remember much ✓

• Vocabulary
Choose five words from the Vocabulary list and read them to a friend. Your friend must write them down, and then make a sentence with each word. Check your friend's sentences.

• Test a friend
Look again at Units 7 and 8. Think of at least two questions, then ask a friend.

"Did Charlie buy a DVD player?"   "Where do U2 come from?"

• Correcting mistakes
Can you correct these mistakes? In some sentences there is more than one mistake.

1 ~~I've bought some fruit at the market yesterday.~~
2 ~~We can play football now. The rain stopped.~~
3 ~~Has ever she be to the USA?~~
4 ~~I didn't see my uncle since three years.~~
5 ~~I know Carla for a long time.~~

• Your Workbook
Complete the Learning Diaries for Units 7 and 8.

Coursework 4 My guidebook

Read Ana's guidebook, then write some useful information on the same topics for a visitor to your country.

Useful information

Have you ever been to the UK? If you haven't, you might find this information helpful.

Postcards and letters

When you go to the post office to buy your stamps, you can say:

I want to send a postcard to Cairo, please.

How much is a stamp for Egypt?

It's easy to see letter boxes in the UK, because they're usually red.

Telephones

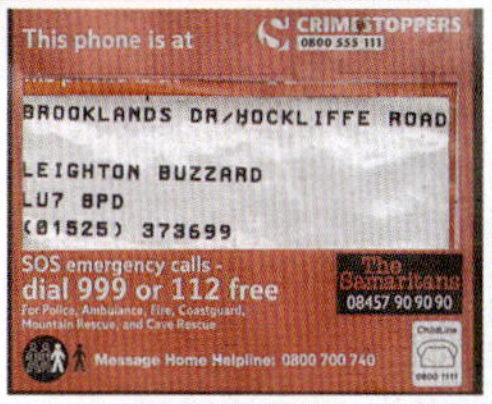

If you want to use a public telephone, you must buy a card, or you can sometimes use coins. Modern telephone boxes are usually grey, but there are still a lot of traditional red telephone boxes, particularly in small towns and in the country. In an emergency, dial 999 for the police, for an ambulance or for the fire service.

Shopping

The shops usually open at 9.00 or 9.30 and close about 5.30. Supermarkets are often open in the evening too. Some shops are open on Sunday. In big towns, there is often a particular day for 'late night shopping', when all the shops are open in the evening.

Changing money

You can change your money at a 'bureau de change', at a bank and sometimes at a travel agent's. In the cities, you might find a 'bureau de change' in the big department stores too.

Somewhere to stay

If you have come to the UK for a visit but you aren't staying with a family, you can stay at a Youth Hostel. There are over 230 in the UK, and seven in London. You can find details on the Internet. Once you have chosen a hostel, you can make a reservation online too.

yha

Getting information

There's a Tourist Information Centre in most towns. Look for this sign. You can get information about events and places, and you'll find maps, brochures, postcards and guidebooks.

Module 5

The way it's done

In Module 5 Steps 1 and 2 you study

Grammar
- *have to, don't have to, mustn't*
- *should/shouldn't*
- Present simple passive
- Past simple passive
- Passive + *by*

Vocabulary
- Illnesses and injuries
- Names of different materials

Expressions
- Thanking people and responding to thanks
- Expressing a reaction

so that you can
- Talk about rules and obligations
- Describe rules at your school and at your ideal school
- Understand and give advice
- Make suggestions when there's a problem
- Describe what things are made of
- Do a general knowledge quiz and make a quiz
- Talk about when and where things are/were made, built or produced

Life and culture

Mardi Gras
Living in an international world

Coursework 5

Part 5 Mini phrase book
You write a mini phrase book for a visitor to your country.

Here are some useful sentences for your

When you are introduced to someone for the first time, if they say:
How do you do?
you should say:
How do you do?

When you say goodbye, you can say:
Bye.
See you soon.
See you later.
See you.

At my school, we usually say:
Good morning or Good afternoon
teachers when we arrive, or, if it's a
Good evening.
You say Good night when you go t

In Step 3 you ...

read
- A quiz about customs around the world
- A description of animated films

study
- Adverbs
- Parts of speech
- Identifying the topic
- Using pronouns and possessive adjectives

so that you can
- Write about customs in your country
- Describe a film you know well

What's it about?

What can you say about the pictures?

Now match the pictures with sentences 1–5.

1 They don't have to go to lessons.
2 We should call an ambulance.
3 It's made of wood.
4 Where was the world's first skyscraper built?
5 *Snow White and the Seven Dwarfs* was made by Walt Disney.

a

b

c

d

e

9 Getting it right

STEP 1

In Step 1 you study
- *have to, don't have to, mustn't*

so that you can
- talk about rules and obligations
- describe rules at your school and at your ideal school

1 Share your ideas

Look at the photos of Sudbury Valley School. What's it like? How is it different from your school?

It's in the country. There's a lot of space outside.

2 Presentation *They don't have to go to lessons!*

a Close your book and listen to Jodie. Does she like her school?

JODIE: Hi! I'm Jodie Styler. I go to Sudbury Valley School in Massachusetts. It's not the same as an ordinary school because here you can choose what you do. You don't have to follow a school timetable. You don't have to do tests and exams. And you don't have to sit in a classroom all day.

But there are rules at my school too, and everyone has to obey the rules! For example, we all have to help with the cleaning.

We make the rules at our School Meetings. All the students can give their opinion, and then we vote. When someone is speaking at a meeting, you mustn't interrupt.

At Sudbury Valley, you have to think for yourself. That's why I like it here.

b Listen again and follow in your book. Then match 1–6 with a–f and make true sentences.

1 Jodie doesn't have to
2 She has to help
3 Students at Sudbury Valley don't have
4 They have to
5 At a meeting you mustn't
6 Everyone has

a with the cleaning.
b interrupt other people.
c to do tests and exams.
d go to all the lessons.
e make their own choices.
f to obey the rules.

3 Key grammar
have to, don't have to, mustn't

a Look at the examples and complete the explanation.

I/You/We/They	have to	obey the rules.
He/She	has to	do the cleaning.

We use .... *or* .... + *verb to describe rules and obligations.*

Have to *and* must *both mean that something is necessary:*
I'm late! I **have to** go. / I **must** go.

G 14, 15

b Look at the examples and complete the explanation with the negative forms of *have to*.

I/You/We/They	don't have to	go to lessons. do exams.
He/She	doesn't have to	

We use .... *or* .... *+ verb to say that something isn't necessary. There is a choice.*

We use mustn't *to describe an obligation, for example, to give an order. There isn't a choice.*
You **mustn't** interrupt. = Don't interrupt!

G → 14, 15

4 Practice

a Make complete sentences, using *has to* or *have to* and one of these verbs.

stay	work	do	wear	leave	shout

1 Jodie *has to leave* the house at 7.30.
2 Martin .... the washing up after dinner.
3 I go out at the weekend but I .... at home during the week.
4 My grandfather can't hear very well so you .... when you talk to him.
5 Sally's a nurse. She often .... at night.
6 A lot of British schoolchildren .... a uniform.

b Look at the notices and complete the sentences with *mustn't* or *don't have to*.

1

You .... swim here.

2

You .... be a member.

3

You .... pay. It's free!

4

You .... take your dog on the beach.

5

You .... talk.

6

You .... wait for a long time.

c **What about you?** Make at least two sentences about things you have to do and things you don't have to do at home. Compare your sentences.

I have to take our dog for a walk every day.
I don't have to do the cooking.

5 Speaking and listening *Making a pizza*

Jodie and her friend Ross are in the kitchen at Sudbury Valley School. They're making a pizza.

a Which of these ingredients do you think they'll use?

1 ham 2 mushrooms
3 fish 4 onion
5 tomato sauce
6 cheese 7 olives
8 salt and pepper

b Listen to the conversation. Check your answers to 5a.

c Listen again, then complete the recipe card.

Student recipe card No. 8

Very quick and easy pizza
by Jodie Styler

Use a ready-made pizza base and a jar of ready-made [1] .... Put the sauce all over the [2] .... Then add some [3] .... You [4] .... cook it first. Next, add lots of [5] .... and, finally, add some pieces of [6] .... Cook it in a hot [7] .... (220°) for about [8] .... minutes.

6 Writing and speaking *An ideal school?*

Use what you know

Write at least three things that you have to do at your school.

We have to study chemistry, and I hate it!

Now imagine your ideal school. Think of things that students don't have to do.

When the weather's nice, we don't have to go to lessons.

Talk about your ideas with the class.

STEP 2

In Step 2 you study
- vocabulary for illness and injuries
- *should, shouldn't*
- thanking people and responding to thanks

so that you can
- understand and give advice
- make suggestions when there's a problem

a

b

1 Key vocabulary
Illness and injuries

Match the sentences with the pictures. You've got three minutes!

1 She feels sick.
2 He's broken his leg.
3 Ow! I've hurt my finger.
4 I've got a sore throat.
5 She's having an injection.
6 She's just fainted.
7 He's got earache.
8 Here's the first-aid box.

c
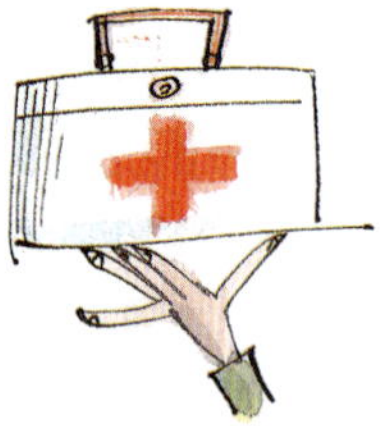

d

e

f

g

h

Listen and check.

Remember!

I've got **a** headache / **a** cold.
I've got toothache/earache/backache/stomach ache.

Try this!

Can you find eight words for parts of the body?
MONTHANDONEYESOARMHAIR
UNOSEATEETHAMOUTHALFACE

2 Presentation *What should we do?*

a Look at the photo. What has happened?

b Close your book and listen. Do Lizzie and the man agree?

Martin, Ana and Lizzie are in the centre of London. A woman has just fainted.

LIZZIE: That woman's fainted!
ANA: She looks terrible! What should we do?
MARTIN: I think we should call an ambulance. I'll ring 999.
MAN: You shouldn't leave her on the ground like that. Let's put her on that seat.
LIZZIE: No, we shouldn't move her.
MAN: I've done a first-aid course, you know. We should put her head between her knees.
LIZZIE: No, we shouldn't.
ANA: Yes, we should! Oh, look ... she's opening her eyes.
WOMAN: Oh ...
MARTIN: It's OK. I've called an ambulance.
WOMAN: Oh, thanks. Thanks very much.
MARTIN: You're welcome. How do you feel?
WOMAN: I feel a bit sick.
LIZZIE: Don't worry. The ambulance will be here in a minute.
WOMAN: Thank you. That's very kind of you.
LIZZIE: No problem. ... I think I can hear it now.

c Listen again and follow in your book. Are these sentences true or false? Correct the false sentences.

1 Lizzie has just fainted.
2 Martin wants to phone the police.
3 The man wants to move the woman.
4 Lizzie thinks that's a bad idea.
5 The man thinks he's a first-aid expert.
6 Lizzie follows his advice.
7 The woman feels fine.
8 An ambulance is coming.

3 Key grammar *should, shouldn't*

Complete the short answers, then complete the explanation.

I/You/He/She We/They	should shouldn't	call an ambulance. move her.

Should Martin ring 999? – Yes, he ______ .
Should I listen to his advice? – No, you ______ .

We use ______ or ______ + verb to ask for and to give advice.

G 16

4 Practice

a Work with a friend. Match problems 1–6 with advice a–f. Complete the advice using the verbs in the box and make six dialogues.

1 I've got a headache.
2 My feet hurt.
3 I've got toothache.
4 I think she's broken her arm.
5 I've got stomach ache.
6 When someone faints, I never know what to do.

do	play	sit	go	eat	take

a You should ______ to the dentist.
b We should ______ her to hospital.
c You should ______ a first-aid course.
d You shouldn't ______ in front of the TV for hours.
e You shouldn't ______ those chips, then.
f You shouldn't ______ football in sandals.

b Test a friend Write another sentence with *should* but leave a blank for the verb. Can your friend complete the sentence?

It's raining. You should ______ your anorak.

c What about you? Think about your bad habits and give yourself some advice! Write your ideas.

I shouldn't leave my clothes on the floor.
I should be nicer to my brother.

Compare your ideas.

5 Key expressions *Thanking people*

a Find four different ways of thanking someone, using these words.

very you thanks thank much

b Work with a friend and make a dialogue.

A: Would you like to sit down?
B: Thank ______ .
That's ______ kind of ______ .
A: That's OK. You're ______ . / No ______ .

If you have time, make another dialogue like this one.

6 Key pronunciation /s/ /ʃ/

a Listen and repeat the words.

1 /s/ Sue see so sore
2 /ʃ/ shoe she show sure

b Now listen to some more words and repeat. Is the sound 1 or 2?

7 Writing and speaking *Problems!*

Use what you know

Work with a friend. Write and practise a short conversation. One person has got a problem. The other person offers advice.

A: Explain the problem. What has happened?
↓
B: Give some advice and offer to help.
↓
A: Say thank you.
↓
B: Respond to A's thanks.

STEP 3

In Step 3 you
- do a quiz about customs around the world
- study adverbs

so that you can
- write about customs in your country

1 Share your ideas *Different customs*

How do you greet people in your country? Can you think of any other customs, for example, what do you say before a meal?

> People in ..... often say ..... before they eat.

2 Reading

a Listen and read the quiz. How many questions can you answer? If you don't know the answer, guess. Then check your score on page 99.

b Comprehension check

Read the quiz again. For each of these sentences write T (true), F (false) or ? (the text doesn't say).

1 If someone says, 'Have you eaten?' when they greet you, they might be Chinese.
2 All over the world people think it's rude to make a noise when you eat.
3 The 'thumbs up' sign sometimes means the number one.
4 Certain customs are the same in every country.
5 In different countries, the same action can have different meanings.
6 If you want to apologise to someone, you can say 'Sorry'.
7 Some colours have got special meanings.
8 When you meet friends in Thailand, you should touch them on the head.
9 In Britain, people don't usually say anything before a meal.
10 Brazilians take flowers to lots of different occasions.

World Travel Guide

Travel Smart

People in different countries often have different customs. If you aren't careful, you might make a mistake and upset someone! Do you know what you should do in these situations?

1 In English-speaking countries, if you accidentally walk into someone, you should smile politely and say ...
- a 'Pardon?'
- b 'Nice to meet you.'
- c 'Sorry.'

2 When you have soup in Japan, to show you like it you should ...
- a eat noisily.
- b burp.
- c lick the bowl when you finish.

3 In China, a popular way to greet someone is to ask ...
- a 'Where have you been?'
- b 'Have you eaten?'
- c 'What are you doing here?'

4 Before they eat, people in Britain usually say ...
- a 'Well done.'
- b 'You're welcome.'
- c nothing.

5 When people in Greece nod their head, they mean ...
- a 'Yes.'
- b 'No.'
- c 'I'm not sure.'

6 In Brazil, you usually take purple flowers when you ...
- a go to a wedding.
- b go to a funeral.
- c visit someone's home for the first time.

7 The 'thumbs up' sign means 'OK!' in Britain, but in Germany it can mean ...
- a 'Go away!'
- b 'I don't agree.'
- c the number one.

8 In Thailand, it's rude to ...
- a shake hands.
- b touch a person on the head.
- c show your teeth when you laugh.

c **Reading skills** *Identifying the topic*
Think about the topic of each question in the quiz, then match it with one of these headings.

Food Particular occasions Language
Physical actions

3 Word work *Adverbs*

Adverbs tell us how something happens.

She speaks ***clearly****.*

We form most adverbs by adding *-ly* to the adjective:

clear > ***clearly****, quick* > ***quickly****, sudden* > ***suddenly***

Some adverbs don't follow this rule:

good > ***well****, fast* > ***fast****, early* > ***early****, late* > ***late***

Remember!

Adjectives ending in -y:
angry > angr**ily**, happy > happ**ily**
Adjectives ending in -l:
careful > careful**ly**, successful > successful**ly**

a Find more adverbs in the quiz.

usually, …

b Write the adverbs for these adjectives.

angry	anxious	bad	calm	careful	easy	
loud	lucky	nice	quick	quiet	sad	slow

angrily, …

c Now choose an adverb from your list in 3b to complete these sentences.

1 'Is that a spider on the floor?' Sue asked ………… .
2 This letter is very important so please read it ………… .
3 'You're two hours late!' Gary's mother shouted ………… .
4 The team played ………… and they lost 4–0.
5 I've got a headache, so please talk ………… .
6 I don't understand. Can you speak ………… , please?
7 'Was it difficult?' 'No, we did it ………… .'
8 Martin made a lot of mistakes because he did his homework too ………… .

Work with a friend and compare your sentences.

Answers to quiz:
1-c, 2-a, 3-b, 4-c, 5-b, 6-b, 7-c, 8-b

Writing guide *Writing an email*

- Write a few words about the topic of your email in the 'Subject line'. For example:
  Your visit
- Begin your email:
  Dear + name
  Young people often use *Hi … , Hello … ,* or *Hey …* + first name with their friends.
- Paragraphs and punctuation
  Use a new paragraph when you write about a new topic.
  Your email will be easier to read if your spelling and punctuation are correct!
- Endings
  Some people use abbreviations like these:
  CU later = See you later.
  BW = Best wishes.
  BFN = Bye for now.

4 Writing *A visit to my country*

Use what you know

Imagine your pen friend is coming to stay with you soon. Write an email describing some of the customs in your country, for example:

Food
When do you usually have breakfast/lunch/dinner?
What do you usually eat?
What special dishes are there in your country?

Language
Think of some useful expressions and explain when you use them.
Do you use the same language when you speak to your friends and when you speak to adults?
What should your pen friend say when he/she meets people for the first time?

Extra exercises

1 Complete the conversations. Use *one* word.

1 A: You look tired. Can I carry your bag for you?
B: Thank you. That's very ________ of you.

2 A: Thank you for all your help.
B: You're ________ .

3 A: Can you help me with my homework?
B: Sure. No ________ .

4 A: Here's your umbrella, sir.
B: Thanks very ________ .

5 A: You've worked very hard today. Thank you.
B: That's ________ . I've enjoyed it.

2 Complete the conversations.

1 What did the head teacher say?
- a We've tidied the classroom.
- b We have to tidy the classroom.
- c We mustn't tidy the classroom.

2 Can I help you to do the washing up?
- a Sit down. You don't have to help.
- b Sit down. You mustn't help.
- c Sit down. You shouldn't help.

3 What's the matter?
- a You should speak with food in your mouth.
- b You shouldn't speak with food in your mouth.
- c You must burp. It's rude.

4 Does Dan know that you're going on holiday?
- a No, should I tell him?
- b Yes, I know he is.
- c No, I've told him.

5 How's your foot? What did the doctor say?
- a I mustn't play sport for a month.
- b I fell down the steps.
- c I should play sport for a month.

3 Complete the sentences with 'illness and injuries' words.

1 Please don't shout. I've got a terrible h________ .
2 Can you stop the car? I feel s________ .
3 I fell over and h________ my arm yesterday.
4 Frank's done a f________ course. He'll help you if you've got a problem.
5 You should go to the dentist if you've got t________ .
6 We ate too much food and now everyone has got s________ .
7 I can't sing very well because I've got a s________ .
8 Sue fainted when the doctor gave her an i________ .

4 Match the questions with the answers.

1 How much homework do you have to do?
2 Can you eat in the classroom?
3 Do you wear a uniform?
4 How much is it?
5 What time shall we leave?

- a Yes, we have to wear a blue jacket and trousers.
- b About two hours every evening.
- c We have to be at the station at 9.00, so let's leave at 8.30.
- d No, we mustn't take food and drink into the classroom.
- e We don't have to pay – it's free.

5 Complete the conversation. Choose from a–h.

A: Mum, I feel ill.
B: 1________
A: I've got a terrible headache.
B: 2________
A: And I've got stomach ache, and I feel sick.
B: 3________
A: But I want to watch TV.
B: 4________
A: OK. I feel really cold, anyway.
B: 5________

- a You should take an aspirin.
- b You look happy!
- c I've done a first-aid course.
- d Cold? I think I'll phone the doctor.
- e You should go to the dentist.
- f You look awful! What's the matter?
- g No, you mustn't watch TV. Go to bed.
- h I think you should go to bed if you feel sick.

6 How do you say these sentences in your language?

1 Your friend looks terrible!
2 You have to think for yourself.
3 Thanks. That's very kind of you.
4 We don't have to wear a uniform at our school.
5 How do you feel?
6 I've done a first-aid course, you know.

Life and culture

Extra reading

Mardi Gras

What festivals are popular in your country or town? Which one do you like best?

People in many parts of the world celebrate Mardi Gras. The name means 'Fat Tuesday' in French. The carnival traditionally started on the day before Ash Wednesday – when Catholics have to stop eating and drinking certain things for Lent. Today, Mardi Gras is a very popular carnival. It begins in January or February and lasts for several days or weeks, until Ash Wednesday. Many people say it is 'the biggest free show on Earth', and it is an exciting holiday for both children and adults.

There are big Mardi Gras celebrations in Rio de Janeiro, Brazil; Sydney, Australia; Nice, France; Venice, Italy; and Cologne, Germany, but the biggest and most famous is in New Orleans, in Louisiana, USA.

In New Orleans the whole city stops for one huge party. Tens of thousands of people fill the streets and there are hundreds of parades. Each parade has a king and queen and people wear very colourful costumes with the Mardi Gras colours of purple, green and gold. There is a lot of music (especially jazz) and dancing. People in the parade throw special Mardi Gras coins, flowers, necklaces and sweets to the crowds. After each parade there is a big party, called a ball. People wear masks and they dance all night. There are always lots of fireworks too.

A favourite tradition of the New Orleans Mardi Gras is the King Cake. This is a special cake in the Mardi Gras colours. There are many different kinds, and people eat thousands of them!

ABOUT NEW ORLEANS

New Orleans is famous for jazz music. Louis Armstrong, the famous jazz musician, came from New Orleans and the airport is called Louis Armstrong International Airport.

Task

Read the text, then answer the questions.

1 What does Mardi Gras mean?
2 Why is it called Mardi Gras?
3 When does the carnival start?
4 When does it finish?
5 Where is the biggest Mardi Gras festival?
6 What do people wear?
7 What kind of music do people play?
8 If you're in the crowd, what might people give you?
9 What happens after each parade?
10 What special food do people eat?

10 Where is it made?

STEP 1

In Step 1 you study
- names of different materials
- present simple passive
- expressing a reaction

so that you can
- describe what things are made of
- talk about where things are produced

1 Key vocabulary *Materials*

Match the words with the photos. You've got two minutes!

silver gold wood cotton
leather glass plastic metal

1

2

3

4
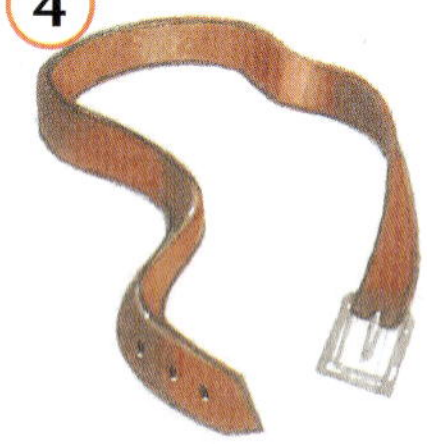

5

6

7

8

Listen and check.

2 Presentation *Is it made in England?*

a What can you say about the photo?

b Close your book and listen to the conversation. How many different things do Ana and Jay look at?

Ana and Jay are at Portobello Road market. It's the largest antiques market in the world. Lots of other things are sold there too.

ANA: I must get some presents for my family. I'm going home next week.

JAY: Yes, I know.

ANA: Clara wants a new watch. These are nice.

MAN: They're only eight quid – a real bargain. They're made in Taiwan.

ANA: Taiwan? They aren't made in England?

MAN: No, love. Everything's imported these days.

ANA: Oh. Well, I'd rather get something English.

JAY: How about this teapot?

ANA: That's nice! How much is it?

JAY: Seventy pounds! That's expensive!

MAN: Don't listen to him, love. It's made of real silver. Look! It's written on the bottom.

JAY: Oh, yes.

ANA: Hey, look! I like these little London buses, Jay.

MAN: A perfect souvenir of England! They're four ninety-nine each.

ANA: Are they made in England?

MAN: I don't think so. Let's see. No, they're made in China. But listen, I'll give you three for ten quid. How about that?

c Listen again and follow in your book. Are these sentences true or false? Correct the false sentences.

1 Only antiques are sold at Portobello Road.
2 Ana wants to buy some souvenirs for her family.
3 The watches are made in London.
4 The man sells things from a lot of different countries.
5 Jay thinks the teapot is a bargain.
6 The teapot is expensive because it's made of silver.
7 Ana might buy some little London buses.
8 She isn't sure because they aren't made in England.
9 The man offers Ana a special price.

3 Key grammar *Present simple passive*

Complete the examples and the explanation with the right form of *be*.

> This teapot **is made** of silver.
> It **isn't made** of gold.
> Things from all over the world .... **sold** at Portobello Road.
> The watches .... **made** in England. They're from Taiwan.
>
> *We form the present simple passive with subject* + is, ..., ..., aren't + *past participle* (made, sold).
>
> *We use the passive when we don't know or aren't interested in who does the action.*
> The watches are made in Taiwan.
> *We don't know who makes the watches.*

G 17

4 Practice

a Look again at the pictures in Exercise 1. Ask and answer questions like these.

A: What's the necklace made of?
B: It's made of silver.

b **What about you?** Describe your things, and things in the classroom. What are they made of?

Our desks are made of plastic and metal.

c Complete the sentences using *is, isn't, are, aren't* + one of these past participles.

spoken	killed	stolen	not used
born	not found		

1 Thousands of mobile phones are stolen every year in the UK.

1 Thousands of mobile phones / every year in the UK
2 The swimming pool in Central Park / in the winter
3 About 350,000 babies / every day
4 Penguins / in the Arctic
5 In Sri Lanka, two people / by poisonous snakes every day
6 English / by about 1.5 billion people

5 Key expressions *Expressing a reaction*

Work with a friend. Read sentences 1–5. Your friend chooses a reaction from a–e.

1 Someone has stolen my new bike.
2 My brother has just won the lottery.
3 Your blood travels 168 million miles every day.
4 These trainers were only $10.
5 Hundreds of tons of food are wasted every day.

a That's fantastic!
b That's cheap!
c That's terrible!
d That's crazy!
e That's amazing!

6 Speaking and writing *Around the world*

Use what you know

Work in groups. Look at the nouns and the past participles. How many true sentences can you make using the present simple passive?

Olives are grown in Greece.
Our rice is imported from China.

cars	coffee	stereos	olives	rice
motorbikes	tea	oranges	grapes	
aeroplanes	racing cars			

grown in	imported from	made in	built in

STEP 2

In Step 2 you study
- past simple passive
- passive + *by*

so that you can
- do a general knowledge quiz, and make your own quiz
- talk about when things were built, made or produced

1 Share your ideas

What do you know about the things and people in the photos?

> I think the painting is called *Sunflowers*. I think it's by Van Gogh.

2 Presentation *Where was it built?*

a Read the quiz and choose the right answer, a, b, or c. If you don't know, guess. You've got five minutes! *1b*

1 Where was the Statue of Liberty made?

a the USA
b France
c Canada

2 Where were the first modern Olympic Games held?

a Rome
b Athens
c San Francisco

3 Where was the world's first skyscraper built?

a London
b New York
c Chicago

4 Which US president was assassinated in 1963?

a Ronald Reagan
b Abraham Lincoln
c John F. Kennedy

5 Where and when was the first lift used?

a in France in 1743
b in Italy in 1853
c in Switzerland in 1895

6 Which famous cartoon character was created by Walt Disney in 1928?

a Spiderman
b Bugs Bunny
c Mickey Mouse

7 Who was the painting *Sunflowers* painted by?

a Picasso
b Monet
c Van Gogh

8 Who were the *Star Wars* films directed by?

a George Lucas
b Steven Spielberg
c Peter Jackson

Listen and check your answers.

Try this!
What is it?
It was built in France in 1889. It isn't a skyscraper but it is still one of the tallest structures in the world.
Can you write a clue like this for something else?

b Are these sentences true or false? Correct the false sentences.

1F It wasn't made in the USA. It was made in France.

1 The Statue of Liberty was made in the USA.
2 The first modern Olympic Games were held in Rome.
3 The world's first skyscraper was built in Chicago.
4 Kennedy was assassinated in 1963.
5 The first lift was used in Italy.
6 Mickey Mouse was created by Walt Disney in 1922.
7 *Sunflowers* was painted by Monet.
8 The *Star Wars* films were directed by Peter Jackson.

3 Key grammar *Past simple passive*

Complete the examples and the explanation.

The first skyscraper **was built** in Chicago.
It **wasn't** .... in New York.
The *Star Wars* films .... **directed** by George Lucas.
They **weren't** .... by Peter Jackson.

We form the past simple passive with ...., wasn't, were, ... *+ past participle.*

We use by *after the passive if we want to say who does/did the action:*
It was painted **by** Van Gogh.

G 17

4 Practice

a Complete the text using the past simple passive.

The world's first computer game [1].......... (*create*) in 1962 by the American Steve Russell. It [2].......... (*call*) *Spacewar* and a huge computer [3].......... (*need*) to play it. The early computers were very expensive so they [4].......... (*not use*) by many people. But in the 1970s computers became smaller and cheaper. *Spacewar* [5].......... (*follow*) by games like *Pong* and *Space Invaders* and thousands of these games [6].......... (*sell*) all around the world.

b **Test a friend** Choose one of the facts from Exercise 2, then put the words in the wrong order. Can your friend say the sentence?

by / 1928 / Disney / was / Mouse / created / in / Walt / Mickey

Mickey Mouse was created by Walt Disney in 1928.

5 Key pronunciation
Weak forms /wəz/ /wə/

Listen and repeat the sentences. Practise the stress, and the weak forms of *was* and *were*.

1 It was /wəz/ **made** in Ame**r**ica.
2 It was /wəz/ **grown** in **Greece**.
3 They were /wə/ **built** in **Brit**ain.
4 They were /wə/ **held** in **Hung**ary.

6 Reading and listening *Song*

a Read about the song *Over the rainbow*. Is the song still famous today?

The song *Over the rainbow* is perhaps the most famous movie song in history. It was written more than half a century ago. It was first sung by Judy Garland in the film *The Wizard of Oz* in 1939.

A number of different singers have recorded the song and, in 2004, it was chosen as 'the best movie song of all time' by the American Film Institute.

Judy Garland's life wasn't a happy one. So the place 'over the rainbow' remained a dream, in her song and in her real life too.

b Now listen to the description of the song. There are five mistakes. What are they?

It wasn't written a century ago. It was written ...

c Listen to the song. Then complete the sentences using these words.

bird dreams fly happy place problems rainbow singer's

1 The song is about a land in the .... dreams.
2 It isn't a real .... It exists on the other side of a ....
3 It's a place where your .... come true.
4 It's a place where everyone is .... and there aren't any ....
5 The singer would like to be a .... , so that she can .... over the rainbow.

7 Writing and speaking *A quiz*

Use what you know

Work with a friend and write at least three more quiz items, using the past simple passive.

Guernica was painted by ...
a Picasso b Michelangelo c Van Gogh

Read your quiz items to the class.

STEP 3

In Step 3 you
- read a description of animated films
- study parts of speech

so that you can
- describe a film you know well

1 Share your ideas
Animated films

How many animated films can you think of? Which ones have you seen? Did you enjoy them?

I like animated films, and I've seen a lot.

2 Reading

a Read the magazine article. What's an 'Annie'?

b Reading skills
Using pronouns and possessive adjectives

Find these phrases and sentences in the text, then read the words or sentences before them. What do the underlined words refer to?

1 *It = the film 'Snow White and the Seven Dwarfs'*

1 It was made in 1937 ...
2 It was released in 1995, ...
3 ... it was an incredible success ...
4 ... the actions and characters in them ...
5 ... he could show a wide variety of emotions.
6 ... made $340 million in its first 25 days ...
7 ... even have their own awards.

The world of computer animation

The world's first full-length animated film was *Snow White and the Seven Dwarfs*. It was made in 1937 by Walt Disney. The images for the early cartoon films were drawn and painted by hand.

The first full-length computer-animated film was *Toy Story*. It was released in 1995, and it was an incredible success with both children and adults. Computers have become much more powerful since the 1990s. In today's films, the most advanced technology is used, so the actions and characters in them have become more and more realistic. For example, in the film *Shrek 2*, Shrek's face had 218 different muscles, so that he could show a wide variety of emotions. But it still takes days, weeks or even months to complete a scene, and it took three years to make *Shrek 2*.

Today, animated films are 'big business'. *Shrek 2* made $340 million in its first 25 days in the USA. Hundreds of artists, computer animators, software developers and engineers are used for each film.

At first, the script isn't recorded by professional actors. The voices are read by the people who are making the film. Later, when the film is nearly finished, famous stars are paid millions of dollars to play the parts of the main characters. Animated films even have their own awards. The 'Best Animated Feature Film' category was introduced in 2002, and the awards are called 'Annies'!

c **Comprehension check**

Listen, and read the text again. Then answer the questions.

1 Were the first cartoons made a long time ago?
2 Did Walt Disney use a computer?
3 How are today's animated films made?
4 Was the film *Toy Story* popular?
5 Have computers changed much since the 1990s? How?
6 Today's animated films are better than the earlier ones. Can you say why?
7 How long can it take to make an animated film?
8 Why do they cost a lot of money?

3 Word work *Parts of speech*

Look at these three different parts of speech:

success (*noun*)
successful (*adjective*)
(to) succeed (*verb*)

Complete the tables. You might need to use a dictionary.

	noun	adjective
1	length	long
2	animation	....
3	....	successful
4	....	powerful
5	width	....

	noun	verb	past participle
6	action	act	acted
7	creation	create	....
8	introduction	....	....
9	drawing	....	....
10	painting	....	....

Writing guide *Describing a film*

- Give a few facts.

  It's an American film. It was made in 1997. It's still very popular.

- Describe the story.

  When we describe the action in a film, we often use the present simple.

  The hero of the film is called Jack. At the beginning of the film he lives in England but then he goes to America on a ship. He meets ... and they ...

- Use link words.

  At the beginning of the film, ...
  Then ... After that ...
  At the end, ...

- Give your opinion.

  I thought it was great but my friend didn't enjoy it very much.

4 Writing and speaking *Famous films*

Use what you know

Think of a film that you know well and write a short paragraph about it. Don't write the name of the film!

Where and when was it made?
Who are the main characters?
What happens at the beginning of the film?
Then what happens?
How does the story end?
What did you think of the film?

Read your description to a friend. Can your friend guess the name? Share your opinions about the film.

Extra exercises

1 Complete the conversations.

1 Peter has broken his leg.
  a That's crazy!
  b That's nice!
  c That's terrible!

2 My dog can understand every word I say.
  a That's awful!
  b That's amazing!
  c That's sad!

3 This coat cost €350.
  a That's nice!
  b That's expensive!
  c That's difficult!

4 I studied all night and didn't go to bed until five o'clock.
  a That's crazy!
  b That's fantastic!
  c That's funny!

5 My parents came to my school and sat next to me in class.
  a That's irritating!
  b That's embarrassing!
  c That's amazing!

2 Complete the sentences. Use these verbs in the present simple passive or past simple passive.

kill make grow write destroy paint sell discover

1 Thousands of trees *are destroyed* every year by pollution.
2 The play *Hamlet* .... by Shakespeare.
3 These rings .... of gold.
4 The Sistine Chapel .... by Michelangelo.
5 The moons of Jupiter .... by Galileo.
6 Many people .... by smoking.
7 A lot of rice .... in China.
8 The Harry Potter books .... in countries all over the world.

3 Make sentences with the past simple passive.

1 Where were the 2004 Olympic Games held?

1 Where / the 2004 Olympic Games / hold / ?
2 My bicycle / steal / last night
3 St Paul's Cathedral / design / by Christopher Wren
4 Why / the pyramids / build / ?
5 Our old house / destroy / by fire
6 The new rules / introduce / last week

4 Complete the second sentence so that it means the same as the first one. Use the right passive form.

1 Lee Harvey Oswald killed President Kennedy.
  President Kennedy *was killed by Lee Harvey Oswald* .
2 My brother writes the software for this computer game.
  The software for this computer game ....
3 They released the new cartoon yesterday.
  The new cartoon ....
4 Several people saw the accident.
  The accident ....
5 People grow a lot of rice in Thailand.
  A lot of rice ....
6 Last night someone stole half a million euros from that bank.
  Half a million euros ....

5 Read the text. Put the letters in order and make seven 'materials' words.

Protecting the environment is important. We should recycle things like [1]*asgls* bottles, and we shouldn't use new [2]*scpiatl* bags every time we go shopping. We can even recycle clothes, so you should take your old [3]*tcotno* shorts and T-shirts the next time you go to the recycling centre. Of course, you can recycle things that are made of [4]*tlame* too. Some people throw away amazing things – I've found [5]*lsvire* jewellery and a [6]*dolg* watch at my local recycling centre!

6 How do you say these sentences in your language?

1 Someone has stolen my ring. – That's awful!
2 It's made of real gold.
3 It's a bargain!
4 They're only two quid.
5 I'll give you three for ten euros.
6 It's a perfect souvenir.

Extra reading

Life and culture

Living in an international world

Make a list of things you often use. Do you know where they were made?

Joanne has never been abroad, but she has a very international life! Every morning for breakfast she drinks a cup of black coffee and eats some melon.

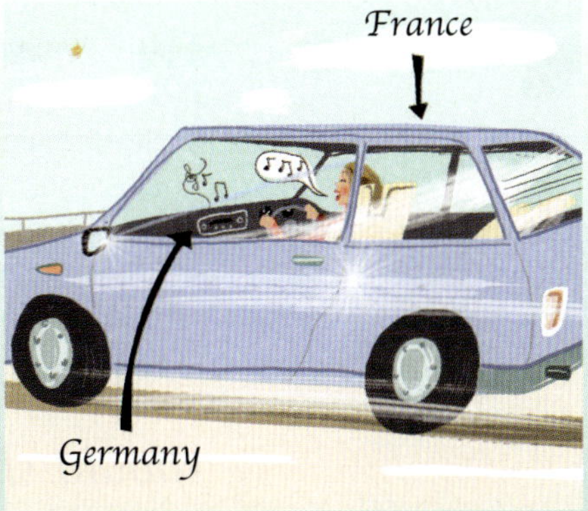

She gets into her car and drives to work. In the car, she listens to music on the radio. If there is a song she knows, she usually sings along with the music.

Joanne is a clothes designer. She really loves her job. She makes coats, using leather and silk. The coats are sold all around the world. She uses a computer in her work and she advertises her coats on the Internet.

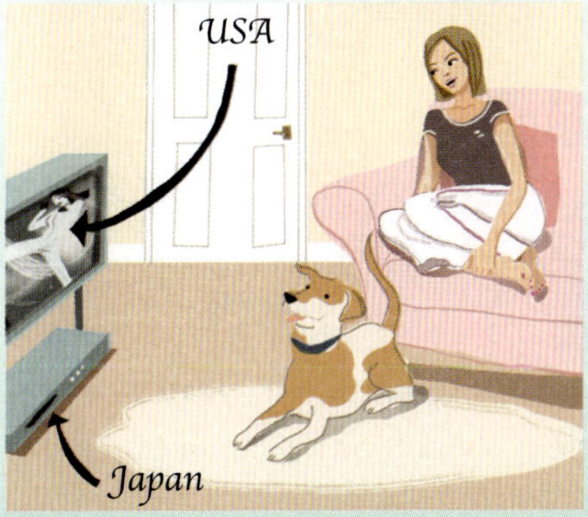

When she gets home after work, she takes her dog for a walk and then cooks dinner. After dinner, she likes watching films on her DVD player.

On Saturday night Joanne goes out with her friend Natasha. They go to a salsa dance class together.

After that, they have an Indian meal in a restaurant with Joanne's boyfriend, Sean.

ABOUT INTERNATIONAL TRAVEL

According to the *Guinness Book of Records*, Robert and Carmen Becker of Florida, USA, have been to almost every country in the world. They can count the places that they haven't visited on one hand.

Task

Read the text, then answer the questions.

1 Where does Joanne's coffee come from?
2 Where was her melon grown?
3 Where was her car produced?
4 Where was her radio manufactured?
5 Where was her computer made?
6 Where is her leather imported from?
7 Where was her DVD player made?
8 Where were her friends Natasha and Sean born?
9 What kind of dancing do they do?

Module 5 Review

Grammar check

1 *have to/don't have to, must/mustn't*

Work it out for yourself

A Match sentences 1–4 with pictures A and B.

1 *I must get up.*
2 *I don't have to get up.*
3 *I have to get up.*
4 *I mustn't stay in bed.*

FRIDAY SUNDAY

B Now match sentences 1–4 with these explanations.

a We use this negative form to describe an obligation or give an order.
b We use this negative form to say that something isn't necessary.
c We use these affirmative forms to say that something is necessary.

Check that you can

1.1 • talk about obligations.

Choose the right answer.

1 I've got toothache. I (*must / mustn't*) go to the dentist.
2 You (*must / mustn't*) sit there. That's 26. Your seat's number 28.
3 I hate Saturday mornings because I (*mustn't / have to*) do the housework.
4 My brother wants to be an ambulance driver. He (*has to / mustn't*) do a first-aid course.
5 You (*must / mustn't*) eat those chocolates. They're Martin's.
6 My sister's going to spend a month in Peru. She (*have to / has to*) have lots of injections.

1.2 • say what is an obligation or what isn't necessary.

Make sentences using *don't/doesn't have to* or *mustn't*.

1 We don't have to put olives on the pizza.

1 We haven't got any olives for the pizza, but that doesn't matter. (*We/put*)
2 The concert's free. (*We/pay*)
3 There isn't a uniform at Jodie's school. (*She/wear*)
4 Students can't take mobile phones into the classroom. It's a rule. (*They/use*)
5 I'd like to be a cat because cats can sleep all day. (*They/work*)
6 Why are you opening that letter? It isn't for you. (*You/read*)

2 *should/shouldn't*

Work it out for yourself

Look at the pictures and answer the questions.

You must go to the doctor.
Look at my thumb! It's black.
You should go to the doctor.

TOM'S MOTHER TOM HARRY

1 Match sentences a and b with pictures 1 and 2.
   a *Why don't you go to the doctor?*
   b *Go to the doctor!*
2 Who is giving advice?
3 Who is giving an order?

Check that you can

• give advice.

Complete the sentences with *should* or *shouldn't*.

1 If you burn your finger, you *should* put it in cold water.
2 You .... have a first-aid box at home.
3 You .... go to the doctor simply because you feel tired.
4 You .... go everywhere on the bus. You .... walk into town.
5 You .... sit in the sun all day.
6 You .... drink lots of water. It's good for you!

3 The passive
Work it out for yourself

A Look at the pictures. Match these descriptions with sentences 1 and 2.

a The sentence describes the action and the person who does the action.
b The sentence only describes the action.
c The sentence doesn't tell us who cleans the car.

1 *Kim **cleans** her car every week.* (active)

2 *The Prime Minister's car **is cleaned** every week.* (passive)

B Match 1 and 2 with a and b.

1 We use a sentence with a passive verb when …
2 We use a sentence with an active verb when …

a we're interested in the action and the person who does it.
b we're more interested in the action than in the person who does it.

Check that you can

3.1 • talk about things that are done or were done.

Put the words in the right order. Write sentences in the passive form of the present simple or the past simple. Use the verbs in brackets.

1 A lot of coffee is grown in Kenya.

1 coffee / lot / a / Kenya / of / in (*grow*)
2 helicopter / first / the / 1939 / in (*build*)
3 all / the / over / world / English (*speak*)
4 Britain / aeroplane / in / the (*not invent*)
5 Pyramids / when / the ? (*build*)
6 email / when ? (*invent*)

3.2 • understand when we use the passive.

Complete the sentences. Put the verbs into the active or passive form of the past simple.

1 Have you heard about Kelly's new bike? It *was stolen* (*steal*) yesterday.
2 You know that Rick wanted to sell his guitar. Well, he .... (*sell/it*) for €120 last week.
3 What happened to the old house in Church Street? – It .... (*sell*) for €385,000 two days ago.
4 Poor James. His dog .... (*kill*) on the road last night.
5 Emma and Chloe are really happy. They .... (*win*) the tennis championship yesterday. They played ten matches and they .... (*not beat*) once!
6 You know Sally's father is a songwriter. Well, one of his songs .... (*perform*) on television last night.

4 The passive + *by*
Work it out for yourself

Look at the two sentences, then answer the question.

*The first electric guitar **was made** in 1928.*
*It **was made by** George Beauchamp.*

We can give extra information after a passive verb. What word do we use to say who did the action?

Check that you can

• use the passive + *by*.

Correct the sentences. Use the names in the box.

Picasso Alexander Bell Bob Dylan
the Egyptians the French

1 No, they didn't. It was built by the French.

1 The Americans built the Statue of Liberty.
2 Marconi invented the telephone.
3 The Romans built the Pyramids.
4 Van Gogh painted *Guernica*.
5 Elvis Presley wrote the song *Blowin' in the wind*.

Vocabulary and expressions

Illness and injuries

ambulance
backache
(to) break (a leg)
earache
(to) faint
(to) feel sick
first-aid (box)
(to) hurt
illness
injection
injury
(a) sore throat
stomach ache
toothache

Thanking people and responding to thanks

Thanks./Thank you.
You're welcome.
That's very kind of you.
No problem.
That's OK.

Customs

(to) apologise
(to) burp
custom
funeral
(to) greet
(to) lick
(to) nod
occasion
polite
(to) shake hands
(to) upset
wedding

Adverbs

angrily
anxiously
badly
calmly
carefully
clearly
early
easily
fast
happily
late
loudly
luckily
nicely
noisily
politely
quickly
quietly
sadly
slowly
successfully
suddenly
well

Materials

cotton
glass
gold
leather
metal
plastic
silver
wood

Expressing a reaction

That's amazing!
That's awful/terrible!
That's cheap!
That's crazy!
That's great/fantastic!
That's interesting!
That's nice!

Animated films

cartoon
character
computer-animated
(to) create
engineer
feature film
full-length
image
realistic
scene
script
software

Study skills 5 Speaking

How many of these things do you do? Score one point for each 'Yes'. Then add up your score. You've got two minutes!

1 When the class repeats something, I always join in.
2 I practise the dialogues in the book with a friend.
3 I work with a partner and ask and answer questions.
4 I talk to my teacher in English when I can.
5 I greet my friends in English at the beginning of the lesson.
6 When we learn a new word, I say it aloud.
7 When we do pairwork, I try to use English all the time.
8 I pretend to have conversations with an English friend.
9 I play my English CD at home and copy the voices.
10 I listen to English songs and I try to sing them.

Score:
5–10 You're making good progress with your speaking.
0–4 Try to do more of the things on the list.

How can you improve your speaking?

I'm going to talk to the teacher in English more often.

How's it going?

Your rating

Look again at pages 110 and 111. For each section decide on your rating: Good ✓✓✓ Not bad ✓✓
I can't remember much ✓

Vocabulary

Look at the Vocabulary list. Choose five words that, in your opinion, are difficult to pronounce. Write them down, then share your ideas and practise saying the words.

Test a friend

Look again at Units 9 and 10. Think of at least two questions, then ask a friend.

Did you like the school in Unit 9?

What was the first animated film?

Correcting mistakes

Can you correct these mistakes? In some sentences there is more than one mistake.

1 ~~You don't have to run in the corridor. You must to walk.~~
2 ~~Listen to her advice. You should must go to the dentist.~~
3 ~~You shouldn't to eat too much. You'll feel sick.~~
4 ~~Edam cheese is make in Holland.~~
5 ~~The Mona Lisa was painting for Leonardo da Vinci.~~

Your Workbook

Complete the Learning Diaries for Units 9 and 10.

Coursework 5 My guidebook

Read Ana's mini phrase book, then make a mini phrase book for a visitor to your country. Remember to put the explanations in English! You should write about other situations too, for example, at the end of a meal or at parties.

Mini phrase book

Here are some useful sentences for your visit to an English-speaking country.

When you are introduced to someone for the first time, if they say:
How do you do?
you should say:
How do you do?

When you say goodbye, you can say:
Bye.
See you soon.
See you later.
See you.

At my school, we usually say:
Good morning or Good afternoon to our teachers when we arrive, or, if it's an evening class, Good evening.
You say Good night when you go to bed.

At a shop or a café, you must remember to ask politely, for example:
Can I have a packet of aspirin, please?
or Could I have a hot chocolate?

When you sit down at the table for a meal, you don't have to say anything. But British people sometimes say:
Enjoy your meal or
Bon appetit.

If you want to apologise, you mustn't say Pardon? (it means What did you say?). Say I'm sorry or I'm so sorry! or I'm awfully sorry! or I'm terribly sorry!

If you want to know where a place is, ask:
Excuse me. Can you tell me the way to the bus station? or Is there a bank near here?

Module 6

The way we live

In Module 6 Steps 1 and 2 you study

Grammar
- Reported speech
- *say* and *tell*
- Question tags
- *used to*
- Second conditional

Vocabulary
- Relationships
- Words from American English

Expressions
- Asking for clarification
- Saying goodbye

so that you can
- Talk about relationships
- Report what other people say
- Ask if something is true or not, or ask for agreement
- Ask for clarification
- Talk about differences between life in Britain and the USA
- Describe things that happened in the past but that don't happen now
- Say goodbye
- Talk about imaginary situations

In Step 3 you ...

read
- A story from the Internet about a telephone conversation
- Some extracts from an encyclopaedia

study
- Verbs that describe speaking
- Punctuation marks
- Synonyms
- Skimming
- Scanning

so that you can
- Write a conversation using the correct punctuation
- Write an essay about your country

Life and culture

Central Park
Living in the past

Coursework 6

Part 6 Entertainment
You write about entertainment in your country.

The most popular TV programmes are quiz programmes and soap operas, *EastEnders* and *Coronation Street*. Some of them have been on TV for a long time. Tim and Penny Grant used to watch *Coronation Street* when t were teenagers.

If you came to the UK f several months, you wo able to join a gym or a c or go to an evening clas There is always a big ch from karate to cooking, first-aid to photography Italian to ecology.

The West End of London is famous its theatres. Going to the theatre h a popular pastime here since the ti Shakespeare. Shakespeare's plays ar difficult to understand, even for En people, but I really like *Romeo and*

What's it about?

What can you say about the pictures?

Now match the pictures with sentences 1–5.

1 He isn't in a very good mood, is he?
2 Mr Grant said Charlie never did anything to help.
3 I didn't use to drive to work.
4 Goodbye. Thanks for having me.
5 If you were a koala, you'd need 22 hours' sleep.

a

b

c

d

e

11 Talking

STEP 1

In Step 1 you study	so that you can
• vocabulary for relationships	• talk about relationships
• reported speech	• report what other people say
• *say* and *tell*	

1 Key vocabulary *Relationships*

a Match the sentences with the pictures. You've got two minutes!

1. My brother really **annoys** me.
2. I **get on well with** my parents.
3. Don't **argue**! Turn that music off now!
4. They're **having a row**.
5. Kelly is Tara's **closest friend**.
6. I love my dog and my dog loves me. We love **each other**.
7. I **spend a lot of time** with my friends.

Listen and check. Practise the sentences.

b **What about you?** Make at least one true sentence using the key vocabulary.

> My brother and sister don't like each other!

2 Presentation
They said they weren't rebels

a Listen to three British teenagers and follow in your book. Are they like teenagers in your country?

Gemma

> I don't think I'm a rebel. I don't often argue with my parents. In fact, my mum's my closest friend.

Dave

> People think teenagers are lazy, but I'm not lazy. I work hard at school and I've got a weekend job too.

> I can't talk to my parents about problems. They don't understand me. But it doesn't really worry me, because I don't spend much time at home.

Donna

b Listen and read the article about teenagers in Britain. Are you surprised by the results of Jane Barker's study?

Talking to today's teens

by **Jane Barker**

Are today's teenagers really lazy, rude and unhelpful? I talked to forty teenagers and their parents. I wanted to find out if they got on well.

Most of the teenagers said that they weren't rebels. For example, Gemma, aged 14, said that she didn't often argue with her parents. She said her mother was her closest friend.

Sixteen-year-old Dave told me that he certainly wasn't lazy. He said that he worked hard at school and he had a weekend job too.

Several teenagers told me they weren't happy at home, but they also said their families were important to them. Donna, aged 15, said that she couldn't talk to her parents about problems because they didn't understand her. But she said it didn't worry her because she didn't spend much time at home!

c Match 1–5 with a–e and make true sentences.

1 Dave said that
2 Dave told
3 Gemma said she
4 Several people told Jane they
5 Most of the teenagers said

a Jane he wasn't lazy.
b that they weren't rebels.
c weren't happy at home.
d didn't often argue with her parents.
e he worked hard at school.

3 Key grammar *Reported speech*

Complete the examples and read the explanation.

Direct speech	Reported speech
Present simple →	Past simple
'I work hard.'	He said (that) he worked hard.
'We don't argue.'	She said (that) they .... argue.
am/is/are →	was/were
'I'm not lazy.'	He said (that) he wasn't lazy.
'They're important.'	She said (that) they .... important.
has/have got →	had
'I've got a job.'	He said (that) he .... a job.
can →	could
'I can't talk to them.'	She said (that) she .... talk to them.

When we report what someone said, we often change the present tense to the past tense.

We sometimes use that *in reported speech, but we often omit it.*
He said **that** he worked hard. *or* He said he worked hard.

G 18

4 Practice

Write sentences with *He/She/They said ...*

1 She said she was fed up.

1 'I'm fed up,' she said.
2 'We're going away,' they said.
3 'I don't know,' he said.
4 'I've got a new car,' she said.
5 'I can speak Chinese,' he said.
6 'I look like my sister,' she said.
7 'I don't often go out,' he said.
8 'We love each other,' they said.

5 Key grammar say *and* tell

Complete the explanation with *say* and *tell*.

She **said** (that) it didn't worry her.
Gemma **told** Jane (that) she liked her mum.
Donna **told** her (that) she wasn't worried.
We use the verbs ..... and ..... to introduce reported speech.
We use ..... when we say who we are talking to.

G 18

6 Practice

Complete the sentences. Use the right form of *say* or *tell*.

1 What did Gemma *tell* you? Did she .... anything about the weekend?
2 She .... me that there was a party on Saturday.
3 Did she .... you where it was?
4 She .... she thought it was at Pete's.
5 But Pete .... me he wasn't having a party.

7 Listening *Don't be so rude!*

a Listen to the conversation. Why is Charlie's dad angry?

b Listen again, then say what happened.

Charlie said he always ...

Charlie offered to ...

8 Writing and speaking *What did they say?*

Use what you know

Think of at least one question about teenage life in your country. Work in a group and ask everyone your question.

Do you like school?

Yes, I love it!

No, I don't.

Note the answers, then report your findings to the class.

STEP 2

In Step 2 you study

- question tags
- *Pardon? Could you say that again? What does ... mean?*

so that you can

- ask if something is true or not, or ask for agreement
- ask for clarification when you don't understand

1 Share your ideas

What can you say about the photo? Does Charlie look happy? Do you remember what happened in Step 1?

Charlie's in a bad mood.

2 Presentation *He isn't in a good mood, is he?*

a Close your book and listen to the conversation. What's the matter with Charlie?

It's Tuesday evening. Ana's talking to Charlie and Penny Grant. They've just finished their dinner.

ANA: You're going out this evening, aren't you?
CHARLIE: No, I'm not.
ANA: But you usually go to karate on Tuesday, don't you?
CHARLIE: Yes, I do, but I'm grounded.
ANA: Pardon? Could you say that again?
CHARLIE: I'm grounded. It means I have to stay at home. Dad said I couldn't go out this week.
ANA: Oh, I see.
MRS GRANT: It's your fault, Charlie. You didn't clean the car, did you? And you weren't very polite, were you?
CHARLIE: I know! Don't worry. I'll hang out with the cat. I'll have a great time, won't I?
MRS GRANT: Oh dear. He isn't in a very good mood, is he?
ANA: No, he isn't. Penny, what does 'hang out' mean?
MRS GRANT: It means 'spend time with someone'. Anyway, why don't we see what's on TV?
ANA: OK. We can hang out together, can't we?

b Listen again and follow in your book. Are these sentences true or false? Correct the false sentences.

1 Charlie's going out this evening.
2 He's going to karate.
3 He can't go out at all this week.
4 It isn't Charlie's fault. He wasn't rude.
5 Charlie doesn't really think he'll have a great evening.
6 Charlie wants to stay at home.
7 Everyone's in a bad mood.
8 At first, Ana doesn't understand the expression 'hang out'.
9 Ana and Mrs Grant are going to spend the evening together.

3 Key grammar *Question tags*

a Read the explanation and complete the examples with the right 'tag'.

We use a negative 'tag' after an affirmative sentence.
We use an affirmative 'tag' after a negative sentence.

You**'re** going out, **aren't** you?
He **isn't** in a very good mood, **is** he?
You **weren't** very polite, ... you?
I**'ll** have a great time, ... I?
We **can** hang out together, ... we?

In sentences in the present simple and past simple, we use do/don't, does/doesn't, did/didn't *in the 'tag':*

You **go** to karate on Tuesday, **don't** you?
You **didn't clean** the car, ... you?

We usually use short answers after sentences with question tags:

You're going out, aren't you?
Yes, I am. / No, I'm not.

G 19

b How do you say these 'tags' in your language?

4 Practice

a Match sentences 1–9 with question tags a–i.

1 Charlie's had a row with his dad,
2 His dad was very angry,
3 Charlie can't go to karate,
4 He's fed up,
5 He went to karate last Tuesday,
6 He doesn't want to stay at home,
7 Ana likes learning new words,
8 She didn't understand 'hang out',
9 Ana and Penny are going to watch TV,

a can he?
b didn't he?
c hasn't he?
d wasn't he?
e aren't they?
f did she?
g isn't he?
h doesn't she?
i does he?

b Now work with a friend and choose at least three sentences from 4a. Make dialogues like this.

Charlie's had a row with his dad, hasn't he?

Yes, he has.

c **Test a friend** Write a sentence with a question tag, then write it again but leave a blank. Can your friend say the complete sentence?

It's Wednesday today, ...

It's Wednesday today, isn't it?

Try this!

Write the sentences.

AN A'SI NTHEK ITCH ENIS N'TS HE?
THE YWAN TTOW ATCHT VDO N'TT HEY?

5 Key expressions *Asking for clarification*

a How do you say these sentences in your language?

Pardon? Could you say that again? What does it mean?

b Put the sentences in the right order, then practise the conversation.

– It's difficult to explain. Have you got a dictionary?
– I said I was feeling a bit stressed out.
– Pardon?
– What does 'stressed out' mean?
– I'm feeling a bit stressed out today.

6 Key pronunciation *Intonation in question tags*

a Listen and repeat the sentences.

1 *You're going out this evening, aren't you?* ↗
Here, Ana isn't sure. She's asking a question, so her voice goes up.

2 *He isn't in a very good mood, is he?* ↘
Here, Mrs Grant isn't really asking a question. She's sure, so her voice goes down.

b You're going to hear five dialogues. Listen and then repeat the question. Does your voice go up (↑) or down (↓)?

7 Speaking *Finding out about a friend*

Use what you know

Work in pairs. Make a conversation about your partner using question tags. If you're sure, your voice goes down at the end. If you don't know the answer, your voice goes up.

A: Your name's Celine, isn't it? ↘
B: Yes, it is.
A: You live in ... , don't you? ↘
B: Yes, I do.
A: You've got two brothers, haven't you? ↗
B: No, I haven't.

Take it in turns to ask and answer. If you didn't hear clearly, or you didn't understand, use expressions from 5a.

STEP 3

In Step 3 you

- read a story from the Internet about a telephone conversation
- study verbs that describe speaking
- revise the names of punctuation marks

so that you can

- write a conversation using the correct punctuation

1 Share your ideas *Telephone talk*

How often do you use the phone? Who do you usually ring? What do you talk about?

I use the phone nearly every day.

2 Reading

a Reading skills *Skimming*

Read the text quickly. You've got one minute!

Now answer these questions. Don't look at the text.

1 This is a conversation ...
   a on television. b on the phone.
2 The boy and girl in the conversation ...
   a know each other. b don't know each other.
3 Who makes the phone call?
   a The girl. b The boy.
4 The boy ...
   a tells the truth. b doesn't tell the truth.
5 Choose two adjectives to describe how the girl feels at the end of the conversation.
   happy upset nervous angry tired

stories

http://www.currentarticles.net/stories

home | stories | images | community

Wrong Number

Last Wednesday night I was watching television when the phone rang.

'Hello?' I said. It was a girl's voice at the other end.

'Can I speak to Ben, please?'

There's no one called Ben in our house. It was probably a wrong number but I was bored. I replied, 'I'm sorry, he isn't in.'

'Do you know what time he'll be back?' she asked.

'I think he'll be home about ten.'

There was a long silence. 'Is that Steve?'

My name isn't Steve either. This was definitely a wrong number. So I replied, 'Yes, it is. Can I take a message for Ben?'

'Well, he said he was staying at home tonight and he asked me to call him,' she said in an irritated voice.

I replied, 'Well, he went out with Karen about an hour ago. He said he was coming back at ten.'

A shocked voice said, 'Who's Karen?!'

'The girl he went out with.'

'I know that! I mean, who is she?'

'I don't know her last name. Look, do you want to leave a message for Ben?'

'Yes. Tell him to call me when he gets home.' She was really angry now.

'Sure. Is that Jennifer?'

She exploded. 'Who's Jennifer?'

'Well, he's going out with Jennifer at ten. I thought you were Jennifer. Sorry. It was a mistake.'

'I think Ben has made the mistake! Tell him that Alice called and I'm very upset and ask him to call me.'

I smiled and said, 'OK, but Becky won't like this ...'

b Comprehension check

Listen, and read the text again. For each sentence write T (true), F (false) or ? (the text doesn't say).

1 The girl on the phone is called Alice.
2 A boy answers the phone. His name is Ben.
3 Alice wants to speak to a boy called Steve.
4 Alice has got the wrong number.
5 The boy pretends his name is Steve.
6 Alice says that Karen is her friend.
7 Jennifer and Karen are sisters.
8 The boy is serious, but the girl is joking.

c Now answer these questions.

1 When did the conversation take place?
2 Why didn't the boy tell the truth?
3 What do you think is the relationship between Ben and Alice?
4 How many different girls did the boy mention?
5 Why was Alice upset?
6 At the end of the conversation, how did the boy feel?

3 Word work *Verbs for 'speaking'*

a Choose one of the verbs from the box to complete these sentences. Use the right form of the verb each time.

ask	shout	reply	tell	say	speak	talk

1 How many different languages can he *speak*?
2 Dave .... her if she could telephone him.
3 Donna .... me she was very worried.
4 I asked Charlie why, but there was silence. He didn't ....
5 My sister was very angry. She .... 'I hate you!' and ran out of the room.
6 Sorry, could you .... that again?
7 Ana and her mother get on really well. They always .... about problems together.

b Test a friend Write another sentence for 3a. Can your friend say the complete sentence?

Can you ..... me the time, please?

Can you tell me the time, please?

Writing guide
Punctuating a conversation

- Note the way we punctuate conversations:

  'Is your name Ben?' I asked.
  'No,' he answered. 'It's Steve.'
  'That's strange,' I said. 'I thought it was Ben.'

- We usually start a new line when a different person is speaking.
- The main punctuation marks are:

. full stop	, comma
? question mark	! exclamation mark
' apostrophe	' ' inverted commas
D capital letter capital 'd'	d small letter small 'd'

4 Writing and speaking
A conversation

Use what you know

Write this conversation using the right capital letters and punctuation.

thephonerangandmariaansweredithelloshesaidhelloisthathannahaboyaskednoitisntmariarepliedithinkyouvegotthewrongnumberohsorrythevoiceattheotherendsaidthatsoknoproblemmariatoldhimgoodbye

How many capital letters, full stops, commas, question marks and inverted commas are there in your conversation? Work with a friend and compare your results.

Extra exercises

1 Choose the right tags.

1 Jodie's bought a guitar, ...
  a isn't she?
  b didn't she?
  c hasn't she?

2 You're stressed out, ...
  a don't you?
  b aren't you?
  c haven't you?

3 They don't want to come to the party, ...
  a don't they?
  b do they?
  c doesn't it?

4 Tony wasn't angry when you rang, ...
  a wasn't he?
  b was he?
  c is he?

5 We'll be able to have a holiday this year, ...
  a won't we?
  b can't we?
  c will we?

2 Complete the conversation with the correct form of *say* or *tell*.

A: So, what did you [1].......... John when you saw him?
B: I [2].......... him I didn't want to see him again.
A: Really! What did he [3].......... ? Was he very upset?
B: He [4].......... me he was sorry. He [5].......... that it wasn't his fault.
A: Oh, he always [6].......... that! Did you have a big row?
B: No, but I won't go out with him again. Don't [7].......... anyone at school.
A: OK. I won't [8].......... a word.

3 Read the text and choose the right word for each space.

Simon is one of my [1].......... friends. I get on [2].......... with him and we [3].......... a lot of time together, but sometimes he [4].......... me, especially when he doesn't listen to me. We never [5].......... for long – we're soon good friends again. In fact, we help [6].......... a lot. I hope we'll always be friends.

1	a nearest	b closest	c worst
2	a good	b nice	c well
3	a take	b use	c spend
4	a annoys	b explains	c admires
5	a argue	b rebel	c explode
6	a each time	b each one	c each other

4 Rewrite these sentences. Use *tell* and reported speech.

1 Nigel told Jason that he was very lucky.

1 Nigel / Jason: 'You're very lucky.'
2 Veronica / Gary: 'I work as a waitress three days a week.'
3 Mum / my brother and me: 'You can't watch TV tonight.'
4 Charles / his wife: 'There's nothing to eat in the fridge.'
5 Mark / Jane: 'I'm not playing tennis tonight.'
6 They / their teacher: 'We aren't confident about the exam.'

5 Rewrite these sentences. Use direct speech.

1 'I'm very tired,' Tom said.

1 Tom said he was very tired.
2 Tina said she was having a party on Saturday night.
3 I said I didn't feel very well.
4 They said they got on well with each other.
5 Brian said he loved adventure films.
6 Helen told Frank she couldn't go out with him.

6 Complete the conversation. Choose from a–h.

A: Could you turn the computer off? That game is very loud.
B: [1]..........
A: I said, 'Could you turn the computer off?'
B: [2]..........
A: No, you're not! You're reading.
B: [3]..........
A: Thanks. Oh, look, you've got an error message.
B: [4]..........
A: It means there's a problem. Click on *open* and I'll have a look.
B: [5]..........
A: Click on *open*. OK, let's have a look.

a I'm reading the instructions. I'll turn the sound off.
b Pardon? What did you say?
c It isn't my fault!
d Could you say that again? Click on ...
e No, I can't turn it off. I'm using it.
f I don't read!
g Oh, what does it mean?
h Thanks for helping me.

7 How do you say these sentences in your language?

1 I'm really fed up – I'm grounded.
2 Why is Peter in a bad mood?
3 Tammy and Karin hang out together a lot.
4 I'm really stressed out today!
5 Don't get angry. I said I was joking.
6 We'll have a great time, won't we?

Extra reading

Life and culture

Central Park

Think of a big park that you know. What can you do there?

Central Park, in Manhattan, is a popular place for people in New York to meet, 'hang out' and have fun. New Yorkers say that the 843-acre park is their own 'front garden', where they can relax and escape from the noise of one of the busiest cities in the world. There are lots of things to do in the park. You can play games, go jogging, cycling, horse-riding, or rollerblading, or simply sunbathe on the grass. You can visit the Metropolitan Museum, and there's even a zoo! There are 58 miles of paths to explore, but don't worry if you get tired; you can have a rest on one of the 9,000 benches. There are outdoor concerts and plays and, if you want something to eat, there are some great restaurants, like The *Tavern on the Green*. Central Park is famous all over the world and around 25 million people visit it each year.

However, the park hasn't always been so popular. When it opened, in 1858, only rich people used it. Poor people said it was too expensive to get there. When transport became cheaper, the park became more popular and, in 1926, the first playground was built. But in the 1960s and 1970s the park became dirty and dangerous, so people didn't want to go there. Then, in 1980, an organisation called The Central Park Conservancy took control and everything changed. They spent millions of dollars on the park. They planted trees and added a lot of new attractions. Now there are 21 playgrounds and there's even a skating rink. It costs $20 million a year to look after Central Park, but most people agree that it's worth it.

ABOUT NEW YORK

New York was originally called New Amsterdam. When the British took the city from the Dutch in 1664, they renamed it after the Duke of York.

Task

Read the text and these sentences. For each sentence, write T (true), F (false) or ? (the text doesn't say). Correct the false sentences.

1. There aren't many gardens in New York.
2. You can't take bicycles into the park.
3. Central Park is a good place for families to visit.
4. There are animals in the park.
5. More tourists than New Yorkers use the park.
6. It's nearly sixty miles from one end of the park to the other.
7. You have to be rich to go to Central Park.
8. The park was more popular in the past than it is today.
9. In the 1970s people were afraid of going into the park.
10. The Central Park Conservancy spend a lot of money on the park.

12 New beginnings

STEP 1

In Step 1 you study
- words from American English
- *used to*

so that you can
- talk about differences between life in Britain and life in the USA
- describe things that happened in the past but that don't happen now

1 Key vocabulary *American English*

British English and American English aren't always the same.
Match the American words under the pictures with the British words in the list. You've got two minutes!

trainers biscuits pavement holiday
shop trousers petrol lift wardrobe

1 vacation

2 sidewalk

3 cookies

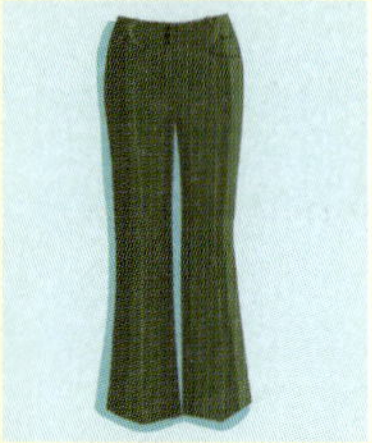
4 pants

5 elevator

6 gas

7 closet

8 sneakers

9 store

Listen and check.

2 Presentation *They used to live in Cardiff*

a Listen to the Richmond family and follow in your book. How many differences between Britain and the USA can you find?

b Read the questions about the Richmonds' life in Britain, then answer them.

1 When she lived in Cardiff, how did Mrs Richmond use to go to work?
2 Did Holly and Seb use to go to school by car?
3 Did Mr Richmond use to be a baseball fan?
4 What sport did he use to like?
5 What did Holly use to wear at school?
6 Did she often go roller blading and swimming?
7 When Seb wanted a packet of 'potato chips', what did he use to say in Britain?

3 Key grammar used to

Complete the examples and read the explanation.

Holly **used to walk** to school but now she goes by car.

Mr Richmond .... **use to like** baseball but now he loves it.

Where **did** they **use to live**? – In Britain.

.... they .... **to live** in Cardiff? – Yes, they did.

We use used to + *verb to talk about a regular activity or a situation in the past that doesn't happen now.*
The negative of used to *is* didn't use to.

We often use never *when we describe things we didn't use to do.*
Holly **never** used to go roller blading.

G 13

4 Practice

a Imagine you're Seb. Make sentences with *used to* and the Key vocabulary from Exercise 1.

1 *In Britain, we used to eat biscuits. In the USA, we eat cookies.*

1 eat ...
2 wear ...
3 put our clothes in ...
4 walk along ...
5 buy ... for the car
6 get ... to the seventh floor
7 buy our food at the local ...

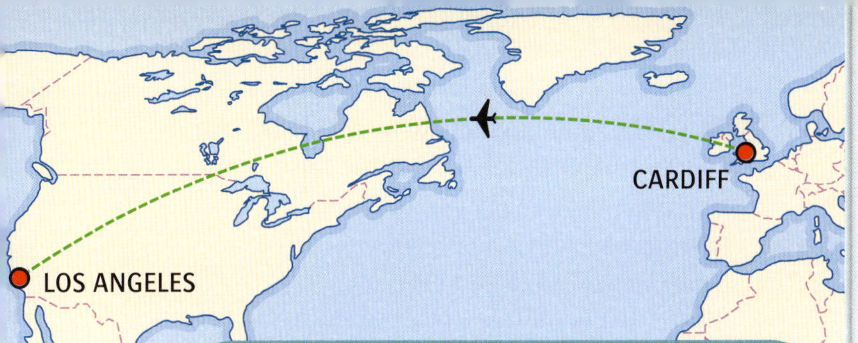

The Richmond family left their home in Cardiff two years ago. They went to live in Los Angeles. We asked them about the differences between their old life in Britain and their life in the USA.

'When we lived in Cardiff, I used to go to work by bus, and the kids used to walk to school. Now we go everywhere by car.'
Mrs Richmond

'I didn't use to be interested in baseball, but everyone's crazy about it here. I used to be a football fan, but now I watch baseball every Saturday.'
Mr Richmond

'In Britain, we used to wear a school uniform. We don't have to wear a uniform here. It's great. What else is different? Well, I didn't use to swim much, but the weather's better here so I often go swimming now. And I never used to go roller blading, but it's really popular here.'
Holly, aged 13

'I used to think the English language was the same everywhere. But it isn't! For example, I used to wear trainers. Here I wear 'sneakers'. We used to eat biscuits. Now we eat 'cookies'. Crisps are called 'potato chips' in the US and chips are called 'fries'!'
Seb, aged 15

b Complete the sentences with *used to* / *didn't use to* + one of these verbs.

live	drive	go out with	like	play	have

1 The Richmonds .... a cat, but they haven't got any pets now.
2 Holly's grandparents .... in Liverpool, but they've just bought a house in Spain.
3 Seb .... a girl called Sandy but he hasn't got a girlfriend at the moment.
4 Mr Richmond .... baseball, but now he's crazy about it.
5 Holly .... hockey at the weekend, but now she goes roller-blading
6 Mrs Richmond .... to work, but now she goes everywhere by car.

5 Listening *Song*

a Close your books and listen. Choose the best description of the song.

It's about ...

a children. b saying goodbye. c memories.

b Listen again, then find the best word to complete these sentences.

1 The singer has gone back to a(n) ... place.
a old b special c strange
2 Her playground was a place where she used to feel ...
a safe. b scared. c lonely.
3 People say you shouldn't think about the ... but the singer doesn't agree.
a future b present c past
4 When she says 'I wish you were here', the singer feels ...
a happy. b sad. c excited.

6 Writing and speaking
I'm different now!

Use what you know

What were you like ten years ago? Write at least three things that are different now, then tell a friend.

I used to have short hair, but now I've got long hair.
I used to believe in ...
I used to like ...

STEP 2

In Step 2 you study
- ways of saying goodbye
- second conditional

so that you can
- say goodbye and thank people after a visit
- talk about imaginary situations

1 Share your ideas

Imagine you've just won an airline ticket. You can choose your destination. Where would you like to go? Why?

I'd like to go to Nepal because I want to see Mount Everest.

2 Presentation
If I had a ticket, I'd go with you now!

a Close your book and listen to the conversation. Who does Ana speak to on the phone?

Ana's going home to Mexico today. She's at the airport with the Grants.

ANA: Goodbye, Penny. Thanks for having me. I've had a great time.
MRS GRANT: Goodbye, Ana. I'll miss you.
ANA: Well, you must come to Mexico one day.
MRS GRANT: I'd like that. If I had a ticket, I'd go with you now!
ANA: Goodbye, Tim. Thanks for all your help.
MR GRANT: No problem. Goodbye, Ana. Keep in touch.
ANA: Yes, of course. Goodbye, Charlie. Would it be OK if I gave you a kiss?
CHARLIE: No, it wouldn't! Bye, Ana. Have a good journey.
ANA: Thanks, Charlie. Be good! And don't argue with your dad!
CHARLIE: If Dad was more easy-going, we wouldn't argue.
MR GRANT: Now wait a minute!
MRS GRANT: Don't start, you two!
ANA: Oh, that's my mobile.
CHARLIE: I bet it's Jay.
ANA: Hi, Jay. I can't speak to you for very long. My flight's leaving soon. ... I'll miss you too ... Bye.

b Listen again and follow in your book. Are these sentences true or false? Correct the false sentences.

1 Ana hasn't enjoyed her stay in London.
2 Penny is happy that Ana is leaving.
3 Penny would like to go to Mexico.
4 Penny can't go with Ana because she hasn't got a ticket.
5 Tim hopes that Ana will contact them soon.
6 Charlie doesn't want a goodbye kiss.
7 Charlie doesn't think his father is very easy-going.
8 He says that's why they argue.
9 Jay has come to the airport to say goodbye.

3 Key grammar *Second conditional*

Read the examples and complete the explanation.

We use the second conditional when we imagine a hypothetical situation in the present or the future:
If Dad **was** more easy-going, we **wouldn't** argue.
(= Dad isn't easy-going, so we argue.)

Sometimes the situation is completely unreal:
If I **had** a ticket, I'**d** go with you.
(= Penny can't go to Mexico because she hasn't got a ticket.)

We form the second conditional using If + ... *simple and* .... / wouldn't + *verb.* ('d = would)

Note the questions and short answers:
Would it **be** OK if I gave you a kiss?
Yes, it **would**. / No, it **wouldn't**.

G 9

4 Practice

a Holly met a boy at a party. She wants to see him again but she doesn't know how to contact him. Match 1–5 with a–e and make complete sentences.

1 If I knew his number,
2 If I had his address,
3 If he had my number,
4 If he went to my school,
5 If he saw me in the street,

a I'd see him every day.
b would he remember me?
c I'd phone him.
d perhaps he'd call me.
e I'd write to him.

b Look at your answers to 4a, then work with a friend. Complete and practise the dialogue.

A: Does Holly know the boy's number?
B: No, she doesn't. If she knew his number, she'd ...
A: Has she got his address?
B: No, she hasn't. If she had ..., she ...
A: Has the boy got Holly's ... ?
B: No, he ... . If he ...
A: Does the boy go to Holly's ... ?
B: No, ... If ...

c Complete the sentences, using the second conditional.

1 If I knew (*know*) his phone number, I'd tell (*tell*) you.
2 If I .... (*live*) in California, I .... (*go*) surfing every weekend.
3 If Charlie .... (*help*) at home, he .... (*get on*) better with his parents.
4 If you .... (*be*) more careful, you .... (*not lose*) things all the time.
5 If Holly .... (*have*) more money, she .... (*buy*) a new mobile.
6 If you .... (*not go*) to bed so late, you .... (*not be*) so tired.
7 If I .... (*go*) to Australia, I .... (*visit*) the Great Barrier Reef.
8 If the rainforest .... (*not exist*), our climate .... (*be*) completely different.

d Practise the conversation. Then make another conversation, changing the underlined words.

A: What would you do if you won a lot of money?
B: I'd <u>put it in the bank</u>. What would you do?
A: I'd <u>go to America to see my cousins</u>.

Try this!
Ana's got six presents for her family in her suitcase. What are they?
KOBO THCAW SCUTIBIS RETSOP
RIMORR ATE

5 Key expressions
Saying goodbye

a At the end of a visit, who says these things?

a the visitor b the host
c the visitor or the host

1 Thanks for having me.
2 I've had a great time.
3 I'll miss you.
4 Keep in touch.
5 Have a good journey.

b Now match sentences 1–5 with these explanations.

a Don't forget to contact us.
b I hope you enjoy your journey.
c Thank you for the time I've spent with you.
d I'll be sad without you.
e I've really enjoyed my visit.

6 Key pronunciation /θ/ /ð/

a Listen and repeat the words.

1 /θ/ thanks three think third
2 /ð/ this there then they

b Now listen to some more words and repeat. Is the sound 1 or 2?

7 Speaking *Imagine ...*

Use what you know

Work with a friend and ask and answer questions like these.

If you were an animal, what would you be?
If you were a famous person, who would you like to be?
If you could meet someone from the past, who would you choose?
If you could live in another country, where would you live?

I'd be a cat, because they have a very easy life.

STEP 3

In Step 3 you
- read some extracts from an encyclopaedia
- study synonyms

so that you can
- write an essay about your country

1 Share your ideas *Finding information*

Where do you look when you want to find information? How many different ways of finding information can you think of?

I sometimes go to the school library.

2 Reading

a Reading skills *Scanning*

Read the text quickly and find answers to these questions. Don't read every word. You've got three minutes!

1 How many hours a day does a koala spend awake?
2 How much rice is grown every year?
3 How many Ford Model T cars were produced?
4 How long would it take to fly to the moon?
5 What is the human body made of?

THAT'S AMAZING!

The average adult spends seven hours asleep every day. But if you were a koala, you would need 22 hours of sleep. Koalas only move around and eat at night. They are sometimes called 'koala bears', but they are not bears. They are marsupials – this means they carry their babies in a pouch. When a koala is born, it is only two centimetres long.

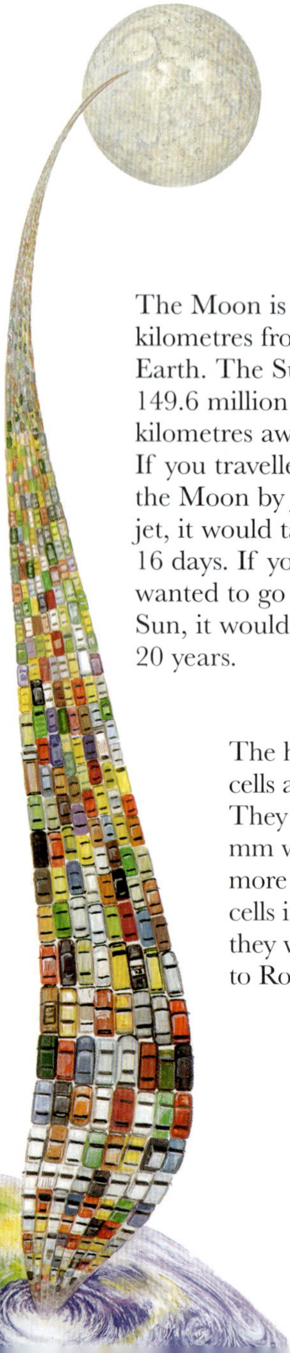

Rice is the main food of over half the world's population. Over 600 million tons of rice is produced every year. If you collected all the rice that people eat in one day, you would have a mountain six times bigger than the Great Pyramid in Egypt.

In 1900 there were 20,000 cars in the world. In 1908 Henry Ford introduced the first mass-produced car, the Model T. Over 15 million were made in total.

Today there are almost 700 million cars. If they all went out at the same time, they would make an eight-lane traffic jam to the Moon.

The Moon is 384,000 kilometres from the Earth. The Sun is 149.6 million kilometres away. If you travelled to the Moon by jumbo jet, it would take 16 days. If you wanted to go to the Sun, it would take 20 years.

The human body is made of cells. Most cells are so small that we cannot see them. They are approximately 0.01 mm to 0.02 mm wide. The average adult body contains more than 100,000 billion cells. If all the cells in a human body were put in a line, they would stretch 1,000 km – from Paris to Rome.

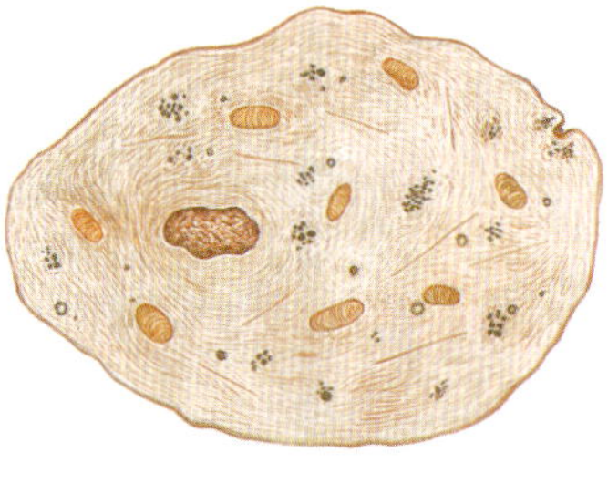

b Comprehension check

Listen, and read the text again. For each sentence write T (true), F (false) or ? (the text doesn't say).

1 Koalas never eat during the day.
2 A bear is a type of marsupial.
3 The Egyptians used to eat rice.
4 More rice is grown than any other food.
5 There were 20,000 Model T cars in 1908.
6 It takes longer to fly to the Sun than to the Moon.
7 It's impossible to see human cells.
8 Everyone's body has got the same number of cells.

c Read the text again. How many 'imaginary situations' are there? Find sentences using the second conditional.

3 Word work *Synonyms*

Synonyms are words which have the same or a similar meaning, for example:

great fantastic wonderful fabulous

a Look at the words in List A and find them in the text. Then use words in List B and make five pairs of synonyms.

A over main almost made approximately
B nearly produced most important about more than

b Now make seven more pairs of synonyms.

annoyed big fantastic certainly unusual large start expensive irritated definitely wonderful strange begin dear

Writing guide *An essay about your country*

- Think of some ideas and make notes. Look back at Units 1–11 and find useful words and ideas. For example:
  - your language (Unit 1)
  - people (Unit 3)
  - places (Unit 4)
  - food (Unit 6)
  - popular activities (Unit 8)
  - customs (Unit 9)
  - things that are produced (Unit 10)
- Plan your essay. Begin a new paragraph for each new topic, or put your topics in groups, for example:
  - population, language, places
  - food and customs
  - people and homes
  - hobbies and popular activities
- Write your ideas in complete sentences. Use the present simple to talk about facts.

  Italy is in southern Europe.
  Most people speak …
- If you want to give your opinion, use *In my opinion* … or *I think (that)* …

  I think Italian people are warm and friendly.

4 Writing *My country*

Use what you know

Write about your country.

What is the population?
Which languages are spoken?
What is the capital city?
Where is the best place to go on holiday?

What sort of food is popular?
Are there any interesting customs in your country?

What are the people like?
What sort of homes do people live in?
What do people do in their free time?

Do you like living in your country, or would you prefer to live somewhere else?

Give your essay to a friend and read your friend's essay. Say what you enjoyed about the essay. Can you find and correct any mistakes?

Extra exercises

1 Complete the conversations.

1 Goodbye Paul. It's been nice to see you.
   a Thanks for telling me.
   b Thanks for waiting.
   c Thanks for having me.

2 Bye! Come again soon.
   a Thank you. How are you?
   b Thanks. I've had a great time.
   c Thanks. I'm having a nice time.

3 I'm leaving now. See you again soon.
   a Have a good journey.
   b You're having a good journey.
   c A good journey!

4 Goodbye. Thanks for everything.
   a I miss you.
   b I'll miss you.
   c I'm missing you.

5 Would it be OK if I wrote to you?
   a Sure. Let's touch.
   b Of course. Let's keep in touch.
   c Certainly. We're in touch.

2 Complete the conversations.

1 How old were you when you .... here?
   a use to come   b used to coming   c used to come

2 .... go to Burnley Grammar School?
   a Were you used to   b Did you use to   c Use you to

3 Bill never .... very easy-going!
   a use to be   b used to be   c was used to being

4 When you were younger, ... argue with your parents a lot?
   a did you use to   b did you used to   c weren't you used to

5 We .... football together every Sunday in the park.
   a use to play   b used to play   c were use to playing

3 Put the letters in the right order and make eight American words (1–8). Then match them with the British words a–h.

1 vacation – f holiday

1 TVAINCOA   2 KICEOOS   3 ESIKADLW   4 NSTPA
5 LTERAVOE   6 TCSLEO   7 SSNEEARK   8 RESOT

a biscuits
b shop
c trousers
d lift
e wardrobe
f holiday
g trainers
h pavement

4 Choose the right words.

1 If I .... a car, I would drive to work.
   a have
   b had
   c 'd have

2 You .... that if your father was here.
   a wouldn't say
   b won't say
   c don't say

3 .... better clothes if I had more money.
   a I buy
   b I've bought
   c I'd buy

4 I'd call him if I .... his number.
   a had
   b didn't have
   c 'd have

5 Do you think .... me with my essay if I asked her?
   a she'd help
   b she'll help
   c she helps

5 Complete the conversation. Use your imagination.

A: What would you do if you found a gold watch?
B: I ....
A: Would you? That's interesting!
B: What .... ?
A: I'd ....
B: Really?

6 How do you say these sentences in your language?

1 Have a good journey.
2 I'd like that.
3 Everyone here's crazy about baseball.
4 Thanks for all your help.
5 Thanks for having me.
6 Don't start, please!

Extra reading

Life and culture

Living in the past

Think about life in your country a hundred years ago. In what ways do you think it was different from life today?

Would you like to go back in time and discover what life used to be like over a hundred years ago? Well, that was the subject of a recent TV programme in the USA. It was called *Frontier House*. Three American families were chosen, from 5,000 applicants, to live in the hills of Montana for five months. The programme was watched by 28 million Americans.

Each family was given their own land (160 acres) and they lived there from June to October. They followed the same way of life as their ancestors over a hundred years ago in the Wild West. They could only use the tools and technology that existed at that time. They learnt many new skills. They became farmers, looking after animals and growing food to eat. They made butter and caught fish.

There was no electricity, so at night they had oil lamps. There was no television and no radio so, in the evening, they read the Bible and talked. They collected wood to do their cooking and to heat their water. They wore the same kind of clothes that people in the 1880s used to wear. Of course, there were no washing machines in those days so they washed all their clothes by hand. When they needed supplies they went ten miles to the store with their horse and wagon. The journey took eight hours.

All the families said that they missed their friends. They couldn't take their mobile phones or their computers with them. They could only write letters. But everyone said they loved their 'new' life and they were all sorry to leave.

ABOUT LIFE IN THE PAST

A hundred years ago in the USA, people washed their hair with egg yolks. Most people only washed their hair once a month.

Task

Read the text, then copy and complete the table.

A hundred years ago, people in the USA:	
used to	didn't use to
be farmers	

Module 6 Review

Grammar check

1 Reported speech

Work it out for yourself

A Look at the verbs in the two sentences. Complete this explanation:

If we use the present tense in direct speech, we often change it to the .... tense in reported speech.

Direct speech

'My sister really **annoys** me.'

Reported speech

Dave said his sister really ***annoyed*** *him.*

B Now look at these sentences. What can you say about the verbs *tell* and *say*, and the word *that*?

1 He said his sister really annoyed him.
2 He said that his sister really annoyed him.
3 He told me his sister really annoyed him.
4 He told me that his sister really annoyed him.

Check that you can

1.1 ● **report what people say.**

Make sentences in reported speech. Start with *He/She/They said ...* .

1 She said (that) she never argued with her parents.

1 SALLY: 'I never argue with my parents.'
2 JACK AND HIS FRIENDS: 'We all get on well with each other.'
3 JAMES: 'My dog's my closest friend.'
4 POLLY: 'I always have a row with my boyfriend at parties.'
5 TOM: 'I don't listen to other people's advice.'
6 MR AND MRS TAYLOR: 'We don't spend much time with our children.'

1.2 ● **use *say* and *tell*.**

Complete the sentences with the right form of *say* or *tell*.

1 A: You didn't *tell* me you couldn't come to my party.
B: Yes, I did. I .... you yesterday.
2 A: Did you .... Ellie that I wanted to see her?
B: Yes, but she .... she didn't want to speak to you.
3 A: Did the doctor .... that you could go back to school?
B: Yes, but I .... him I still had a headache.
4 A: I .... my parents I was going out, but I didn't .... them where I was going.
B: Did you .... you were going to be late?

2 Question tags

Work it out for yourself

A Match sentences 1 and 2 with explanations a and b.

1 *Brrr! It's cold this morning,* ***isn't it?***

2 *You* ***haven't*** *had a row,* ***have you?***

We use question tags ...
a to ask a question about something when we aren't sure.
b to ask for agreement about something when we are sure.

B Look at sentences 1 and 2 in A and answer these questions.

1 What sort of tag do we use after a negative sentence?
2 What sort of tag do we use after an affirmative sentence?

C Look at these examples, then complete the explanations.

Charlie ***was*** *very rude,* ***wasn't he?***
You ***haven't got*** *a coat,* ***have you?***
You ***can't*** *play the piano,* ***can*** *you?*
He ***won't*** *be able to go out,* ***will he?***
The restaurant ***opens*** *at 7.00,* ***doesn't it?***
You ***don't eat*** *fish,* ***do you?***
Kate ***went*** *to London yesterday,* ***didn't she?***
She ***didn't go*** *by train,* ***did she?***

1 After *be*, *have*, *can* and .... , we use the same verb in the question tag.
2 After a present simple verb (*opens*), we use *do/*.......... or ....*/doesn't* in the question tag.
3 After a past simple verb (*went*), we use .... or *didn't* in the question tag.

Check that you can

- make sentences with question tags.

Complete the sentences with the right tag.

1 You like Tanya, *don't you* ?
2 You don't wear glasses, ______ ?
3 You didn't come to school yesterday, ______ ?
4 You haven't been to America, ______ ?
5 You went out with James last night, ______ ?
6 Maria's nice, ______ ?
7 The exam was difficult, ______ ?
8 'Stressed out' means 'anxious', ______ ?
9 Your parents weren't very pleased, ______ ?
10 We can meet outside the cinema, ______ ?

3 *used to*

Work it out for yourself

Match sentences 1 and 2 with explanations a–d. (One of the explanations goes with both sentences.)

1 I played basketball. 2 I used to play basketball.

a The speaker is talking about the past.
b It's clear that this was a regular activity in the past.
c We can add the word *yesterday* to this sentence.
d Things have changed and the speaker doesn't play basketball now.

Check that you can

3.1 • make sentences with the different forms of *used to*.

Put the words in the right order and make sentences.

1 I didn't use to like mushrooms.

1 use / mushrooms / didn't / like / I / to
2 you / live / where / use / to / did ?
3 comics / used / I / to / read
4 never / to / drink / used / I / coffee
5 scared / be / dogs / of / you / did / use / to ?
6 use / glasses / I / wear / didn't / to

3.2 • talk about things in the past that are different now.

Complete the sentences with the right form (affirmative, negative or question) of *used to*.

1 Goran's quite old now, but he's still good at tennis. He *used to play* (*play*) for his country.
2 You've changed! You've got long hair. You ______ (*have*) long hair.
3 I love Indian food now, but I ______ (*like*) it.
4 I haven't got a camera now, but I've got hundreds of photos. Photography ______ (*be*) my hobby.
5 You speak French very well. ______ (*you/live*) in France?

4 The second conditional

Work it out for yourself

Look at the two pictures. Match the sentences in pictures A and B with explanations 1 and 2.

First conditional (present + *will*)

A
If you touch it, it'll bite you.

Second conditional (past simple + *would*)

B
If you touched it, it would bite you.

1 The speaker is imagining a hypothetical situation – it isn't very probable.
2 The speaker is talking about a real possibility – it might happen.

Check that you can

- describe hypothetical situations.

Make sentences in the second conditional.

1 If I had a dog, I'd call it Bonzo.

1 You haven't got a dog, but you think Bonzo is a good name for a dog. (*have/call*)
2 You want to go to the concert, but the tickets cost €50. You haven't got €50. (*have/buy*)
3 You want to go out tonight, but you've got a lot of homework. (*not have/go out*)
4 You've never seen a ghost, but you aren't scared when you imagine the situation. (*see/not be*)
5 You can do your English homework because you use a dictionary. (*not use/not able to*)

Vocabulary and expressions

Relationships
(to) annoy
(to) argue
closest friend
(to) get on well with someone
(to) have a row
(to) like/love each other
rebel
relationship
(to) spend time with

Asking for clarification
Pardon?
Could you say that again?
What does it mean?

On the phone
(to) be back
(to) be in
(to) leave a message
phone call
(to) reply
(to) ring
wrong number

Verbs for speaking
(to) ask
(to) reply
(to) say
(to) shout
(to) speak
(to) talk
(to) tell

Punctuation
apostrophe
capital letter
comma
exclamation mark
full stop
inverted commas
question mark
small letter

Words from American English
(British English meanings in brackets)
closet (= wardrobe)
cookies (= biscuits)
elevator (= lift)
fries (= chips)
gas (= petrol)
pants (= trousers)
potato chips (= crisps)
sidewalk (= pavement)
sneakers (= trainers)
store (= shop)
vacation (= holiday)

Saying goodbye
(to) give someone a kiss
I'll miss you.
I've had a great time.
Thanks for having me.
Keep in touch.
Have a good journey.

Synonyms
about – approximately
almost – nearly
annoyed – irritated
big – large
certainly – definitely
expensive – dear
fantastic – wonderful
made – produced
main – most important
over – more than
start – begin
unusual – strange

Study skills 6 Checking your work

When you write something, it's a good idea to read it afterwards and check for mistakes. Look at the types of mistake in List A, then match them with the sentences in List B.

A	B
1 grammar	a I dont watch cartoons.
2 vocabulary	b I think ʎ is too difficult.
3 word order	c My brother's an enginer.
4 punctuation	d I like very much this exercise.
5 spelling	e I'm going to the library to buy a book for my friend.

Now look at something that a friend has written. How many mistakes can you find? For each mistake, give an explanation and write the correct form. For example:

He's got a very interesting ideas.
grammar: He's got some …

How's it going?

• Your rating

Look again at pages 132 and 133. For each section decide on your rating: Good ✓✓✓ Not bad ✓✓ I can't remember much ✓

• Vocabulary

Choose five words from the Vocabulary list, then write a sentence with each word. Remember to check all the things in the list in Study skills 6.

• Test a friend

Look again at Units 11 and 12. Think of at least two questions, then ask a friend.

Does Charlie Grant get on well with his father?

Is Ana going to stay in England?

• Correcting mistakes

Can you correct these mistakes? In some sentences there is more than one mistake.

1 ~~Dave told he wasn't lazy~~.
2 ~~She said me she were sorry~~.
3 ~~You go to karate, doesn't you~~?
4 ~~They didn't used to go to my school~~.
5 ~~What would do you if you have a million dollars~~?

• Your Workbook

Complete the Learning Diaries for Units 11 and 12.

Coursework 6 My guidebook

Read Ana's guidebook, then write some useful information about entertainment for a visitor to your country.

Entertainment

How will you spend your free time when you're in the UK? Here are some suggestions.

There are lots of different radio stations and TV channels here. I like listening to BBC Radio 1, a pop music channel. I also like Radio 4; there are some really interesting programmes.

The most popular TV programmes are quiz programmes and soap operas, like *EastEnders* and *Coronation Street*. Some of them have been on TV for a very long time. Tim and Penny Grant used to watch *Coronation Street* when they were teenagers.

If you came to the UK for several months, you would be able to join a gym or a club or go to an evening class. There is always a big choice – from karate to cooking, from first-aid to photography, from Italian to ecology.

The West End of London is famous for its theatres. Going to the theatre has been a popular pastime here since the time of Shakespeare. Shakespeare's plays are difficult to understand, even for English people, but I really like *Romeo and Juliet*.

At the weekend, teenagers in London can go to the Trocadero at Piccadilly Circus. There are cinemas, games, shops, rides and 'dodgems'.

There are lots of music festivals in the UK. The most famous is the Glastonbury Festival, which takes place at the end of June. Many of the world's best bands have played there. In London, there are concerts in the parks in the summer.

If you want to know what's happening in London, buy the magazine *Time Out*, or *What's on in London*.

Grammar index

	Unit/Step	Review	Workbook Grammar notes
Adverbs *Can you speak **slowly**, please?*	9.3	5	
As ... as *Is he **as** good-looking **as** you?*	3.2	2	25
Comparatives *London is **bigger than** Paris.*	3.1	2	25
Expressions of quantity *There's **too much** traffic. / There are **too many** people. / There aren't **enough** good shops.*	4.2	2	23
First conditional *You'll be ill if you eat all that.*	6.1	3	8
Have to/don't have to *You **have to** think for yourself.*	9.1	5	14, 15
Infinitive of purpose *They started a campaign **to protect** the environment.*	7.3	4	
Mustn't *You **mustn't** interrupt at a meeting.*	9.2	5	15
Passive			
• present simple *Everything's **imported** these days.*	10.1	5	17
• past simple *The first Olympic Games **were held** in Greece.*	10.2	5	17
Past continuous *He **was studying** physics at Cambridge University.*	2.2	1	4
Past continuous and past simple *I **was waiting** for the bus when I **saw** Tom.*	2.2	1	4
Past simple *I **went** to the cinema but you **weren't** there.*	2.1, 2.2	1	3
Present continuous *It's **raining** outside.*	1.2, 5.1	1, 3	2
Present continuous for the future *We're **getting** the plane at 9.45.*	5.1	3	6
Present perfect *You've **destroyed** thousands of animals and plants.*	7.1, 7.2, 8.1, 8.2	4	11
• with *ever* and *never* ***Have** you **ever travelled** at 2,800 kph? I've **never tried** zorbing.*	8.1	4	11
• with *for* and *since* ***We've been** here **for** five minutes.*	8.2	4	11
• with *just* ***I've just driven** a racing car.*	8.1	4	11
Present perfect and past simple *I've **bought** a DVD player. I **bought** it yesterday.*	7.2	4	12
Present simple *He **comes** from Liverpool.*	1.2	1	1
Question tags *He isn't in a very good mood, **is he**?*	11.2	6	19
Questions and answers *Do you live in Mexico City? No, I don't.*	1.1	1	
Reported speech *Gemma said her mother was her closest friend.*	11.1	6	18
Say* and *tell *He **said** he wasn't lazy. He **told her** he wasn't lazy.*	11.1	6	18
Second conditional *If I had a ticket, I'd go with you.*	12.2	6	9
Should/shouldn't *You **shouldn't** sit in front of the TV for hours.*	9.2	5	16
Suggestions *Why don't we go on the London Eye?*	4.1	2	22
Superlatives *I'm **the best** player in the school.*	3.1	2	25
The future with *going to* *He's **going to** buy a present for his girlfriend.*	5.1	3	7
The future with *might* *You **might** be ill.*	6.2	3	10
The future with *will/won't* *I **won't** be a minute.*	5.2, 6.1, 6.2	3	5
Used to *I **used to** go to work by bus.*	12.1	6	13
***Will* in offers** *I'**ll** carry that for you.*	5.2	3	5
Will/won't be able to *He **won't be able to** eat all that.*	6.1	3	5

Communicative functions index

Unit 1

- Greet people *How do you do?*
- Introduce people *This is Tom.*
- Ask questions when you meet people *Where are you from?*
- Describe place of birth and nationality *I come from Veracruz. I'm Mexican.*
- Talk about your daily life *I have breakfast at 7.00.*
- Talk about what someone is doing *Ana's getting up.*

Unit 2

- Talk about events in the past *I left the flat at seven.*
- Apologise *I'm sorry.*
- Accept an apology *Don't worry about it.*
- Describe a situation in the past *It was raining.*

Unit 3

- Compare and describe two things *Basketball is more exciting than football.*
- Compare one thing with the rest of a group *I'm the tallest person in my family.*
- Talk about differences and similarities *His hair isn't as curly as mine.*
- Ask about appearance *What does she look like?*
- Ask about personality *What's she like?*
- Describe personality *He's very easy-going and he's honest.*

Unit 4

- Make suggestions *How about taking a boat trip?*
- Respond to suggestions *That's a nice idea.*
- Describe a place you know *There aren't enough cafés.*
- Say what you like and dislike about a place *I think it's boring here.*

Unit 5

- Talk about future arrangements *We're meeting outside the school at 12.00.*
- Talk about future intentions *We're going to raise a lot of money.*
- Make decisions *I think I'll try it on.*
- Make offers *I'll hold your bag.*
- Ask for things in a shop *Can I try this on?*

Unit 6

- Talk about results *If I don't help, she'll be angry.*
- Make polite requests *Could you pass me the bread, please?*
- Talk about food in a restaurant *I think I'll try the soup.*
- Make promises *I'll send you lots of letters and emails.*
- Talk about future probability *It might rain later.*

Unit 7

- Describe achievements *People have travelled to the moon.*
- Describe changes *She's changed the colour of her hair.*
- Talk about what you've done and when you did it *I've done my homework. I did it before dinner.*
- Talk about using a machine *Have you plugged it in?*
- *I think so. I don't think so.*

Unit 8

- Talk about experiences *I've never climbed a mountain.*
- Describe things that happened a short while ago *They've just got off the plane.*
- Ask how long present situations have continued *How long have you known Otto?*
- Say how long present situations have continued *I haven't seen you for ages.*

Unit 9

- Talk about obligations *You have to be a member.*
- Describe things that aren't necessary *You don't have to do tests and exams.*
- Give advice *You should go to the dentist.*
- Thank someone *Thank you. That's very kind of you.*
- Respond to thanks *You're welcome.*

Unit 10

- Describe what things are made of *It's made of leather.*
- Talk about where things are/were made or produced *They're made in Taiwan.*
- Express a reaction *That's amazing!*
- Talk about who did something *It was painted by Van Gogh.*

Unit 11

- Talk about relationships *I get on well with my parents.*
- Report what people say *They said they weren't rebels.*
- Ask if something is true or not *You've got two brothers, haven't you?*
- Ask for agreement *It's hot today, isn't it?*
- Ask for clarification *Could you say that again?*

Unit 12

- Talk about things that no longer happen *We used to go to football matches.*
- Say goodbye after a visit *I'll miss you.*
- Thank people after a visit *Thanks for having me.*
- Talk about imaginary situations *If you were more careful, you wouldn't lose things.*

Wordlist

Abbreviations *adj* = adjective *Amer* = American English *n* = noun *prep* = preposition *v* = verb
colloq = colloquial 1.2 = Unit 1, Step 2 CW1 = Coursework, Module 1

A

about (= approximately) /ə'baʊt/ 12.3
abroad /ə'brɔːd/ 1.3
accidentally /ˌæksɪ'dentəli/ 9.3
achieve /ə'tʃiːv/ 7.3
achievement /ə'tʃiːvmənt/ 5.3
add /æd/ 9.1
admire /əd'maɪə/ 5.3
adopt /ə'dɒpt/ 7.3
advantage /əd'vɑːntɪdʒ/ 3.1
adventure /əd'ventʃə/ 2.3
adventurous /əd'ventʃərəs/ 3.2
advertisement / advert /əd'vɜːtɪsmənt 'ædvɜːt/ 7.1
(be) afraid of /ə'freɪd ɒv/ 5.3
after /'ɑːftə/ 2.3
AIDS /eɪdz/ 8.3
aim (*n*) /eɪm/ 7.3
airline /'eəlaɪn/ 12.2
alarm clock /ə'lɑːm klɒk/ 6.3
album /'ælbəm/ **8.3**
all the time /ɔːl ðə taɪm/ 4.3
alone /ə'ləʊn/ 1.3
almost /'ɔːlməʊst/ 6.3
ambitious /æm'bɪʃəs/ 5.3
ambulance /'æmbjələns/ 9.2
American /ə'merɪkən/ 1.2
angrily /'æŋgrəli/ 9.3
annoy /ə'nɔɪ/ 3.2
annoyed /ə'nɔɪd/ 3.3
antiques /æn'tiːks/ 10.1
anxiously /'æŋkʃəsli/ 9.3
apologise /ə'pɒlədʒaɪz/ 9.3
apology /ə'pɒlədʒi/ 2.1
apostrophe /ə'pɒstrəfi/ 11.3
approximately /ə'prɒksɪmətli/ 12.3
aquarium /ə'kweəriəm/ 4.1
Argentina /ˌɑːdʒn'tiːnə/ 1.2
Argentinian /ˌɑːdʒn'tɪniən/ 1.2
argue /'ɑːgjuː/ 11.1
arrangements /ə'reɪndʒmənts/ 5.1
arrow /'ærəʊ/ 2.3
art gallery /ɑːt 'gæləri/ 4.1
artificial intelligence /ˌɑːtɪ'fɪʃl ɪn'telɪdʒns/ 6.3
artist /'ɑːtɪst/ 4.2
as (a first language) /æz/ 1.3
as well /əz wel/ 4.3
ask /ɑːsk/ 11.3
aspirin /'æsprɪn/ CW5
assassinate /ə'sæsɪneɪt/ 10.2
Australia /ɒs'treɪliə/ 1.2
Australian /ɒs'treɪliən/ 1.2
awake /ə'weɪk/ 12.3
award (*n*) /ə'wɔːd/ 8.3

B

backache /'bækeɪk/ 9.2
(be) bad at /bæd ət/ 5.3
badly /'bædli/ 9.3
(pizza) base /beɪs/ 9.1
basmati rice /bæ'smɑːti raɪs/ 6.1
be back /biː bæk/ 11.3
be in /biː ɪn/ 11.3
bed and breakfast /bed ənd 'brekfəst/ 4.2
before /bɪ'fɔː/ 2.3
(the Friday) before last /bɪ'fɔː lɑːst/ 8.2
begin /bɪ'gɪn/ 12.3
below /bɪ'ləʊ/ 2.3
big /bɪg/ 12.3
(a) billion /'bɪliən/ 1.3
biography /baɪ'ɒgrəfi/ 8.3
biscuits /'bɪskɪts/ 12.1
boots /buːts/ 5.2
bow /bəʊ/ 2.3
branch /brɑːntʃ/ 2.3
break (a leg) /breɪk/ 9.2
Britain /'brɪtn/ 1.2
British /'brɪtɪʃ/ 1.2
brochure /'brəʊʃə/ CW4
bungee-jumping /'bʌndʒi dʒʌmpɪŋ/ 8.1
burp (*v*) /bɜːp/ 9.3
bus stop /bʌs stɒp/ 6.3
business /'bɪznəs/ 1.3

C

cafeteria /ˌkæfə'tɪəriə/ 4.3
calm /kɑːm/ 9.3
calmly /'kɑːmli/ 9.3
campaign (*n*) /kæm'peɪn/ 7.3
campaign (*v*) /kæm'peɪn/ 8.3
Canada /'kænədə/ 1.2
Canadian /kə'neɪdiən/ 1.2
canoeing /kə'nuːɪŋ/ 8.1
capital letter /'kæpɪtl 'letə/ 11.3
captain /'kæptɪn/ 3.3
car park /kɑː pɑːk/ 6.3
carefully /'keəfəli/ 9.3
carrot /'kærət/ 6.1
cartoon /kɑː'tuːn/ 10.2
castle /'kɑːsl/ 4.1
category /'kætəgəri/ 10.3
cathedral /kə'θiːdrəl/ 4.1
cave /keɪv/ CW2
cell (= in the body) /sel/ 12.3
(the nineteenth) century /'sentʃəri/ 8.2
certainly (= definitely) /'sɜːtnli/ 11.1
Certainly! (= Of course!) /'sɜːtnli/ 6.1
chairman /'tʃeəmən/ 6.3
channel (= on TV) /'tʃænl/ 7.3
character (in a book/film) /'kærəktə/ 10.2
charity /'tʃærəti/ 5.1
chat (*v*) /tʃæt/ CW2
chips /tʃɪps/ 12.1
classmate /'klɑːsmeɪt/ 4.3
(the) cleaning /'kliːnɪŋ/ 9.1
clever /'klevə/ 3.2
click (on) /klɪk/ 3.3
climbing /'klaɪmɪŋ/ 8.1
closest (friend) /'kləʊsɪst/ 11.1
closet (*Amer*) /'klɒzɪt/ 12.1
coffee maker /'kɒfi 'meɪkə/ 6.3
coin /kɔɪn/ 2.2
collect /kə'lekt/ 12.1
comma /'kɒmə/ 11.3
common /'kɒmən/ 6.3
communicate /kə'mjuːnɪkeɪt/ 1.3
computer-animated /kəm'pjuːtə 'ænɪmeɪtɪd/ 10.3
computer chip /kəm'pjuːtə tʃɪp/ 6.3
confident /'kɒnfɪdənt/ 3.2
connect /kə'nekt/ 1.3
contact (*v*) /'kɒntækt/ 3.3
contain /kən'teɪn/ 12.3
cookies (*Amer*) /'kʊkiz/ 12.1
cotton /'kɒtn/ 10.1
country /'kʌntri/ 1.2
(a) couple of days /'kʌpl ɒv deɪz/ 8.2
course /kɔːs/ 9.2
crash (*v*) /kræʃ/ 2.2
crawl /krɔːl/ 8.3
create /kri'eɪt/ 10.2
crime story /kraɪm 'stɔːri/ 2.3
crisps /krɪsps/ 12.1
crocodile /'krɒkədaɪl/ 4.2
culture /'kʌltʃə/ 1.3
custom /'kʌstəm/ 9.3
customer /'kʌstəmə/ 8.1
cut (*v*) /kʌt/ 2.3
cycle /'saɪkl/ 5.1

D

(the) day before yesterday /deɪ bɪ'fɔː 'jestədeɪ/ 8.2
dear (= expensive) /dɪə/ 12.3
deckchair /'dektʃeə/ CW2
definitely /'defɪnətli/ 11.3
department store /dɪ'pɑːtmənt stɔː/ 4.1
dessert /dɪ'zɜːt/ 6.1
destroy /dɪ'strɔɪ/ 7.3
details /'diːteɪlz/ CW4
determined /dɪ'tɜːmɪnd/ 7.3
develop /dɪ'veləp/ 6.3
dining room /'daɪnɪŋ ruːm/ 6.3
director /daɪ'rektə/ 6.3
discovery /dɪ'skʌvəri/ 2.2
dish /dɪʃ/ 9.3
DIY (= Do it yourself) /ˌdiː aɪ'waɪ/ CW1
dodgems /'dɒdʒəmz/ CW6
drive (someone) mad /draɪv mæd/ 5.3
dwarf /dwɔːf/ 10.3

E

each other /iːtʃ 'ʌðə/ 1.3
earache /'ɪəreɪk/ 9.2
earn /ɜːn/ 3.1
easily /'iːzəli/ 9.3
easy-going /'iːzi 'gəʊɪŋ/ 3.2
edge /edʒ/ 8.1
(not) either /'iːðə/ 11.3
elevator (*Amer*) /'elɪveɪtə/ 12.1
(What) else? /els/ 12.1
embarrassing /ɪm'bærəsɪŋ/ 3.3
emotion /ɪ'məʊʃn/ 10.3
endangered /ɪn'deɪndʒəd/ 7.3
engineer /ˌendʒɪ'nɪə/ 10.3
English-speaking /'ɪŋglɪʃ 'spiːkɪŋ/ 1.3
Enjoy your meal. /ɪn'dʒɔɪ jɔː miːl/ CW5
enormous /ɪ'nɔːməs/ 8.1
enough /ɪ'nʌf/ 4.1
enter (a competition) /'entə/ 5.3
especially /ɪ'speʃəli/ 5.3

evening class
/'iːvnɪŋ klɑːs/ CW6
event /ɪ'vent/ 2.1
everyone else
/'evriwʌn els/ 3.1
exclamation mark
/ˌekskləˈmeɪʃn mɑːk/ 11.3
exhausted /ɪg'zɔːstɪd/ 2.3
exhibition /ˌeksɪ'bɪʃn/ 4.1
expensive /ɪk'spensɪv/ 12.3
expert (*adj*) /'ekspɜːt/ 5.2
expert (*n*) /'ekspɜːt/ 6.3
explain /ɪk'spleɪn/ 2.1
explode /ɪk'spləʊd/ 11.3
extra /'ekstrə/ 4.3
extraordinary /ɪk'strɔːdnri/ 8.1

F

faint /feɪnt/ 9.2
fall (*v*) /fɔːl/ 2.2
fall asleep /fɔːl ə'sliːp/ 2.3
fame /feɪm/ 8.3
fantastic /fæn'tæstɪk/ 12.3
fantasy /'fæntəsi/ 2.3
feature film /'fiːtʃə fɪlm/ 10.3
feel sick /fiːl sɪk/ 9.2
(a) few weeks /fjuː wiːks/ 8.2
field /'fiːld/ 8.3
fight (*v*) /faɪt/ 8.3
finally /'faɪnəli/ 2.3
find out /faɪnd aʊt/ 11.1
finger /'fɪŋgə/ 9.2
first-aid /'fɜːst eɪd/ 9.2
fish (*v*) /fɪʃ/ 2.3
fitting room /'fɪtɪŋ ruːm/ 5.2
five-star /faɪv stɑː/ 4.2
flight /flaɪt/ 5.1
fly (*v*) /flaɪ/ 2.2
for ages /fər 'eɪdʒɪz/ 8.2
forget /fə'get/ 2.1
forgetful /fə'getfl/ 5.3
fork /fɔːk/ 6.1
form (= document) /fɔːm/ 2.2
formal /'fɔːml/ 1.1
France /frɑːns/ 1.2
French /frentʃ/ 1.2
friendly /'frendli/ 3.2
fries (*Amer*) /fraɪz/ 12.1
Frisbee™ /'frɪzbi/ CW2
full stop /fʊl stɒp/ 11.3
full-length /ˌfʊl'leŋθ/ 10.3
fun /fʌn/ 4.3
funeral /'fjuːnərəl/ 9.3

G

gas (*Amer*) /gæs/ 12.1
generous /'dʒenərəs/ 3.2
get dressed /get drest/ 4.3
get home /get həʊm/ 4.3
get into /get 'ɪntə/ 4.3
get off (the bus) /get ɒf/ 2.1
get on (the bus) /get ɒn/ 4.3
get on well (with someone)
/get ɒn wel/ 11.1
get out of /get aʊt əv/ 4.3
get ready /get 'redi/ 4.3
get to /get tə/ 4.3
get up /get ʌp/ 4.3
give (someone) a kiss
/gɪv ə kɪs/ 12.2
glass (= of water) /glɑːs/ 6.1
glass (= material) /glɑːs/ 10.1
go away /gəʊ ə'weɪ/ 9.3
go clubbing /gəʊ 'klʌbɪŋ/ 6.2
go down /gəʊ daʊn/ 8.1
goal /gəʊl/ 5.3
goat /gəʊt/ 4.2
goggles /'gɒglz/ 5.2
gold /gəʊld/ 10.1
golf course /'gɒlf kɔːs/ 4.2
(be) good at /gʊd ət/ 5.3
good-looking /ˌgʊd'lʊkɪŋ/ 3.2
grass /grɑːs/ 2.3
(the) greatest /'greɪtɪst/ 3.3
great-grandfather
/ˌgreɪt'grændˌfɑːðə/ 8.2
Greece /griːs/ 1.2
Greek /griːk/ 1.2
greet /griːt/ 9.3
grounded (*colloq*)
/'graʊndɪd/ 11.2
grow /grəʊ/ 12.3
grow up /grəʊ ʌp/ 6.3
guide book /gaɪd bʊk/ CW1
guys (colloq) /gaɪz/ 5.1
gym /dʒɪm/ CW6

H

hairdresser /'heəˌdresə/ CW3
(a) half /hɑːf/ 1.3
hang out (*colloq*)
/hæŋ aʊt/ 11.2
hard-working
/ˌhɑːd'wɜːkɪŋ/ 3.2
hatchet /'hætʃɪt/ 2.3
heart attack /hɑːt ə'tæk/ 2.3
hectares /'hekteəz/ CW2
helper /'helpə/ CW2
high jump /haɪ dʒʌmp/ 5.3
high school /haɪ skuːl/ 8.3
high jumper /haɪ 'dʒʌmpə/ 5.3
hit (*n*) /hɪt/ 8.3
hit (*v*) /hɪt/ 2.2
hold /həʊld/ 5.2
hold (the Olympic Games)
/həʊld/ 10.2
holiday /'hɒlədeɪ/ 12.1
home page /'həʊm peɪdʒ/ 1.3
(be/feel) homesick
/'həʊmsɪk/ 1.1
honest /'ɒnɪst/ 3.2
host /həʊst/ 12.2
hot chocolate
/hɒt 'tʃɒklət/ CW5
How about?
/haʊ ə'baʊt/ 4.1
huge /hjuːdʒ/ 8.3
(a) hundred /'hʌndrəd/ 1.3
hurt /hɜːt/ 9.2

I

I bet /aɪ bet/ 8.2
I don't mind.
/aɪ dəʊnt maɪnd/ 4.1
I guess (= I suppose)
/aɪ ges/ 5.3
I'd rather (go shopping)
/aɪd 'rɑːðə/ 4.1
I'm awfully sorry!
/aɪm 'ɔːfli 'sɒri/ CW5
iceberg /'aɪsbɜːg/ 2.2
ideal (*adj*) /aɪ'dɪːəl/ 9.1
illness /'ɪlnəs/ 9.2
image /'ɪmɪdʒ/ 10.2
imaginary /ɪ'mædʒɪnəri/ 12.2
imagine /ɪ'mædʒɪn/ 6.3
import (*v*) /ɪm'pɔːt/ 10.1
improve /ɪm'pruːv/ 6.3
in fact /ɪn fækt/ 11.1
in particular /ɪn pə'tɪkjələ/ 5.3
including /ɪn'kluːdɪŋ/ 8.3
incredibly /ɪn'kredəbli/ 2.3
independent
/ˌɪndɪ'pendənt/ 3.2
informal /ɪn'fɔːml/ 1.1
injection /ɪn'dʒekʃn/ 9.2
injured /'ɪndʒəd/ 7.3
injury /'ɪndʒəri/ 9.2
intelligence /ɪn'telɪdʒns/ 6.3
(be) interested in
/'ɪntrəstɪd ɪn/ 5.3
international /ˌɪntə'næʃnl/ 1.3
introduce (a new product)
/ˌɪntrə'djuːs/ 10.3
inventor /ɪn'ventə/ 2.2
inverted commas
/ɪn'vɜːtɪd 'kɒməz/ 11.3
irritated /'ɪrɪteɪtɪd/ 12.3
irritating /'ɪrɪteɪtɪŋ/ 5.3
Italian /ɪ'tæljən/ 1.2
Italy /'ɪtəli/ 1.2
item /'aɪtəm/ 5.2

J

Japan /dʒə'pæn/ 1.2
Japanese /ˌdʒæpn'iːz/ 1.2
jar /dʒɑː/ 9.1
jewellery /'dʒuːəlri/ CW3
jumbo jet
/'dʒʌmbəʊ dʒet/ 12.3
jump (*v*) /dʒʌmp/ 2.2
junior /'dʒuːniə/ 5.3

K

karate /kə'rɑːti/ 11.2
Keep in touch!
/kiːp ɪn tʌtʃ/ 12.2
kick-off /'kɪkɒf/ 5.1
kid (*colloq*) /kɪd/ 7.3
kiosk /'kiːɒsk/ CW4
kiss (*n*) /kɪs/ 12.2
knife /naɪf/ 2.3
known as /nəʊn æz/ 8.3
koala /kəʊ'ɑːlə/ 12.3

L

laboratory /lə'bɒrətri/ 6.3
land (*n*) /lænd/ 10.2
land (*v*) /lænd/ 2.2
lane /leɪn/ 12.3
large /lɑːdʒ/ 12.3
lazy /'leɪzi/ 3.2
lead singer /liːd 'sɪŋə/ 8.3
leather /'leðə/ 10.1
leave a message
/liːv ə 'mesɪdʒ/ 11.3
letter box /'letə bɒks/ CW4
lick /lɪk/ 9.3
lift (*n*) /lɪft/ 10.2
like (= such as) /laɪk/ 1.3
like / love each other
/laɪk lʌv iːtʃ 'ʌðə/ 11.1
links /lɪŋks/ 3.3
listen to /'lɪsn tuː/ 5.3
live (*adj*) /laɪv/ 8.3
location /ləʊ'keɪʃn/ 2.2
lonely /'ləʊnli/ 12.1
(a) long time /lɒŋ taɪm/ 8.2
(a) long way /lɒŋ weɪ/ 5.1
(have a) look /lʊk/ 5.2
look like /lʊk laɪk/ 3.2
look round (the shops)
/lʊk raʊnd/ 4.1
lottery /'lɒtəri/ 10.1
loudly /'laʊdli/ 9.3
luckily /'lʌkɪli/ 9.3

M

made of /meɪd ɒv/ 10.1
main course /meɪn kɔːs/ 6.1
malaria /mə'leəriə/ 6.2
mark (= in an exam) /mɑːk/ 3.2
marsupial /mɑː'suːpiəl/ 12.3
mass-produced
/ˌmæsprə'djuːst/ 12.3
matching /'mætʃɪŋ/ 3.2
mate /meɪt/ 3.1
material (wood, etc.)
/mə'tɪəriəl/ 10.1
medal /'medl/ 5.3

medium (size) /ˈmiːdiəm/ 5.2
mend /mend/ 7.2
menu /ˈmenjuː/ 6.1
metal /ˈmetl/ 10.1
Mexican /ˈmeksɪkn/ 1.2
Mexico /ˈmeksɪkəʊ/ 1.2
midnight /ˈmɪdnaɪt/ 4.3
(a) million /ˈmɪljən/ 1.3
miss (*v*) /mɪs/ 6.2
(I don't) mind /maɪnd/ 4.1
mobile phone
/ˈməʊbaɪl fəʊn/ 6.3
moody /ˈmuːdi/ 3.2
mosque /mɒsk/ 4.1
mosquito /məˈskiːtəʊ/ 6.2
motorbike /ˈməʊtəbaɪk/ 5.1
mousse /muːs/ 6.1
movie (*Amer*) /ˈmuːvi/ 3.3
muscle /ˈmʌsl/ 10.3
museum /mjuːˈziːəm/ 4.1

N

nearby /ˌnɪəˈbaɪ/ 3.3
nearly /ˈnɪəli/ 12.3
neck /nek/ 9.2
neighbour /ˈneɪbə/ 4.2
newsletter /ˈnjuːzˌletə/ 7.3
nicely /ˈnaɪsli/ 9.3
nod /nɒd/ 9.3
noise /nɔɪz/ 2.3
noisily /ˈnɔɪzɪli/ 9.3
normal /ˈnɔːml/ 4.3
numerous /ˈnjuːmərəs/ 8.3

O

obey /əˈbeɪ/ 9.1
occasion /əˈkeɪʒn/ 9.3
ocean /ˈəʊʃn/ 7.1
olive /ˈɒlɪv/ 9.1
(this) one /wʌn/ 5.2
one and a half
/wʌn ənd ə hɑːf/ 1.3
(the green) ones /wʌnz/ 5.2
opal /ˈəʊpl/ 4.2
optician /ɒpˈtɪʃn/ CW3
order (a meal) /ˈɔːdə/ 6.1
ordinary /ˈɔːdnri/ 4.3
(the) outback /ˈaʊtbæk/ 4.2
oven /ˈʌvn/ 6.3
over (= more than) /ˈəʊvə/ 1.3
over (= finished) /ˈəʊvə/ 2.3
own (*adj*) /əʊn/ 6.3

P

packed lunch /pækt lʌntʃ/ 4.3
painting /ˈpeɪntɪŋ/ 2.1
pair (of sunglasses) /peə/ 7.2
palace /ˈpæləs/ 4.1
panic /ˈpænɪk/ 2.3
pants (*Amer*) /pænts/ 12.1
Pardon? /ˈpɑːdn/ 12.2
pass (= to give) /pɑːs/ 6.1
passenger /ˈpæsɪndʒə/ 2.3
pastime /ˈpɑːstaɪm/ CW6
pâté /ˈpæteɪ/ 6.1
pavement /ˈpeɪvmənt/ 12.1
pay (*v*) /peɪ/ 4.3
payment /ˈpeɪmənt/ 2.2
pen friend /pen frend/ 5.1
pepper /ˈpepə/ 6.1
percent /pəˈsent/ 1.3
perfect (*adj*) /ˈpɜːfɪkt/ 4.2
perform /pəˈfɔːm/ 8.3
performance /pəˈfɔːməns/ 5.3
personal assistant
/ˈpɜːsnl əˈsɪstənt/ 6.3
petrol /ˈpetrəl/ 12.1
phone call /fəʊn kɔːl/ 11.3
phrase book /freɪz bʊk/ CW5
physics /ˈfɪzɪks/ 2.2
pier /pɪə/ CW2
plaice /pleɪs/ 6.1
plan (*n*) /plæn/ 1.2
plant (*v*) /plɑːnt/ 7.3
plastic /ˈplæstɪk/ 10.1
plate /pleɪt/ 6.1
playground /ˈpleɪgraʊnd/ 12.1
plug in /plʌg ɪn/ 7.2
point to /pɔɪnt tuː/ 6.3
poisonous /ˈpɔɪzənəs/ 4.2
Poland /ˈpəʊlənd/ 1.2
policeman /pəˈliːsmən/ 4.1
Polish /ˈpəʊlɪʃ/ 1.2
polite /pəˈlaɪt/ 9.3
politely /pəˈlaɪtli/ 9.3
pollute /pəˈluːt/ 7.1
pop star /pɒp stɑː/ 6.3
popular /ˈpɒpjələ/ 3.3
potato chips (*Amer*)
/pəˈteɪtəʊ tʃɪps/ 12.1
pouch /paʊtʃ/ 12.3
predict /prɪˈdɪkt/ 6.3
prediction /prɪˈdɪkʃn/ 6.3
problem /ˈprɒbləm/ 11.1
produce (*v*) /prəˈdjuːs/ 7.1
promise (*n*) and (*v*)
/ˈprɒmɪs/ 6.2
protect /prəˈtekt/ 7.3
punctuation
/ˌpʌŋktʃuˈeɪʃn/ 11.3
purple /ˈpɜːpl/ 9.3
put in /pʊt ɪn/ 7.2
puzzle /ˈpʌzl/ CW3

Q

(a) quarter /ˈkwɔːtə/ 1.3
question mark
/ˈkwestʃən mɑːk/ 11.3
quickly /ˈkwɪkli/ 9.3
quid (*colloq*) /kwɪd/ 10.1
quietly /ˈkwaɪətli/ 9.3

R

rabbit /ˈræbɪt/ 2.3
rainbow /ˈreɪnbəʊ/ 10.2
rainforest /ˈreɪnˌfɒrɪst/ 7.3
raise money /reɪz ˈmʌni/ 5.1
(I'd) rather /ˈrɑːðə/ 4.1
ready-made /ˌrediˈmeɪd/ 9.1
realistic /ˌrɪːəˈlɪstɪk/ 10.3
reappear /ˌriːəˈpɪə/ 2.3
rebel /ˈrebl/ 11.1
regular /ˈregjələ/ 12.1
regularly /ˈregjələli/ 6.2
relationship /rɪˈleɪʃnʃɪp/ 11.1
release (a record) /rɪˈliːs/ 8.3
remain /rɪˈmeɪn/ 10.2
reply (*v*) /rɪˈplaɪ/ 11.3
(the) rest of (my life)
/rest ɒv/ 6.2
result (*n*) /rɪˈzʌlt/ 1.3
ride (*n*) /raɪd/ CW6
riding /ˈraɪdɪŋ/ CW2
robot /ˈrəʊbɒt/ 6.3
(have a) row /raʊ/ 11.1
rugby /ˈrʌgbi/ CW2
(the) 'rush hour' /rʌʃ aʊə/ CW1

S

sadly /ˈsædli/ 9.3
sail (*v*) /seɪl/ 2.2
sailing /ˈseɪlɪŋ/ 8.1
salt /sɒlt/ 6.1
satellite /ˈsætəlaɪt/ 7.1
say /seɪ/ 11.3
scale (*v*) /skeɪl/ 8.3
scene /siːn/ 10.3
science fiction
/saɪəns ˈfɪkʃn/ 2.3
scientific /ˌsaɪənˈtɪfɪk/ 1.3
script /skrɪpt/ 10.3
scuba-diving
/ˈskuːbə daɪvɪŋ/ 8.1
season /ˈsiːzn/ 8.3
secondary school
/ˈsekəndri skuːl/ 3.1
selfish /ˈselfɪʃ/ 7.1
serviette /ˌsɜːviˈet/ 6.1
several (years) /ˈsevrəl/ 8.2
shake /ʃeɪk/ 2.3
shake hands /ʃeɪk hændz/ 9.3
shape /ʃeɪp/ 3.2
shelter /ˈʃeltə/ 2.3
shocked /ʃɒkt/ 11.3
shop /ʃɒp/ 12.1
shorts /ʃɔːts/ 5.2
shout (*v*) /ʃaʊt/ 11.3
Shut up! /ʃʌt ʌp/ 8.2
shy /ʃaɪ/ 3.2
sidewalk (*Amer*)
/ˈsaɪdwɔːk/ 12.1
silence /ˈsaɪləns/ 11.3
silver /ˈsɪlvə/ 10.1
sink (*v*) /sɪŋk/ 2.2
(the right) size /saɪz/ 5.2
skateboarding
/ˈskeɪtbɔːdɪŋ/ 8.1
slowly /ˈsləʊli/ 9.3
small letter /smɔːl ˈletə/ 11.3
smart (= clever) /smɑːt/ 6.3
sneakers (*Amer*) /ˈsniːkəz/ 12.1
snowboarding /ˈsnəʊbɔːdɪŋ/ 8.1
soap opera /ˈsəʊpˌɒprə/ CW6
socks /sɒks/ 5.2
software /ˈsɒftweə/ 10.3
somewhere /ˈsʌmweə/ 4.1
sore throat /sɔː ˈθrəʊt/ 9.2
souvenir /ˌsuːvənˈɪə/ 10.1
Spain /speɪn/ 1.2
Spanish /ˈspænɪʃ/ 1.2
speak /spiːk/ 11.3
spear /spɪə/ 2.3
spend time with (someone)
/spend taɪm wɪð/ 11.1
spiral /ˈspaɪrəl/ 3.2
spoon /spuːn/ 6.1
sports facilities
/spɔːts fəˈsɪlətiz/ 4.2
square (shape) /skweə/ 3.2
stadium /ˈsteɪdiəm/ 4.1
stamp (*n*) /stæmp/ CW4
stare /steə/ 3.1
starter (food) /ˈstɑːtə/ 6.1
starve /stɑːv/ 7.1
(I'm) starving /ˈstɑːvɪŋ/ 6.1
statistics /stəˈtɪstɪks/ 1.3
statue /ˈstætʃuː/ 10.2
stay (= visit) (*n*) /steɪ/ 12.2
stay with (someone)
/steɪ wɪð/ 1.1
still (*adv*) /stɪl/ 4.3
stomach ache
/ˈstʌmək eɪk/ 9.2
store (*Amer*) (*n*) /stɔː/ 12.1
strange /streɪndʒ/ 12.3
(be) stressed out (colloq)
/strest aʊt/ 11.2
stretch /stretʃ/ 12.3
stupid /ˈstjuːpɪd/ 3.3
success /səkˈses/ 8.3
successful /səkˈsesfl/ 5.3
suddenly /ˈsʌdənli/ 2.3
suggest /səˈdʒest/ 4.1
suitcase /ˈsuːtkeɪs/ 12.2
supergroup /ˈsuːpəgruːp/ 8.3
surface /ˈsɜːfɪs/ 2.3
surfing /ˈsɜːfɪŋ/ 8.1
survive /səˈvaɪv/ 2.3

swimming trunks
/'swɪmɪŋ trʌŋks/ 5.2
swimsuit /'swɪmsuːt/ 5.2
synonym /'sɪnənɪm/ 12.3

T

tablet /'tæblət/ 6.2
take action /teɪk 'ækʃn/ 7.3
take care of /teɪk 'keər əv/ 7.3
take out /teɪk aʊt/ 7.2
(It) takes (five minutes)
/teɪks/ 3.3
talk (*v*) /tɔːk/ 11.3
(apple) tart /tɑːt/ 6.1
teapot /'tiːpɒt/ 10.1
technology /tek'nɒlədʒi/ 1.3
teeth /tiːθ/ 9.3
tell /tel/ 11.3
temple /'templ/ 4.1
term /tɜːm/ 7.2
thanks to /θæŋks tə/ 8.3
That's funny. /ðæts 'fʌni/ 2.1
theatre /'θɪətə/ 4.1
theme park /θiːm pɑːk/ 4.1
then /ðen/ 2.3
(a) thousand /'θaʊznd/ 1.3
three quarters
/θriː 'kwɔːtəz/ 1.3
thumb /θʌm/ 9.3
tidy (*adj*) /'taɪdi/ 3.3
timetable /'taɪmˌteɪbl/ 9.1
toothache /'tuːθeɪk/ 9.2
tracksuit /'træksuːt/ 5.2
traffic /'træfɪk/ 4.2
traffic jam /'træfɪk dʒæm/ 6.3
trainers /'treɪnəz/ 12.1
travel agent
/'trævl 'eɪdʒənt/ CW3
triangle /'traɪæŋgl/ 3.2
trousers /'traʊzəz/ 12.1
truth /truːθ/ 11.3
try on /traɪ ɒn/ 5.2
(the) tube /tjuːb/ CW1
turn off /tɜːn ɒf/ 7.2
turn on /tɜːn ɒn/ 7.2
two point seven five
/tuː pɔɪnt 'sevn faɪv/ 1.3

U

unfriendly /ʌn'frendli/ 3.3
unhelpful /ʌn'helpfl/ 11.1
unkind /ʌn'kaɪnd/ 3.3
unplug /ʌn'plʌg/ 7.2
unpopular /ʌn'pɒpjələ/ 3.3
untidy /ʌn'taɪdi/ 3.3
until /n'tɪl/ 2.1
unusual /ʌn'juːʒuəl/ 12.3
upset (*v*) /ʌp'set/ 9.3
(be) upset (*adj*) /ʌp'set/ 11.3
(the) USA /ˌjuːes'eɪ/ 1.2

V

vacation (*Amer*) /və'keɪʃn/ 12.1
variety /və'raɪəti/ 10.3
volunteer (*n*) /ˌvɒlən'tɪə/ 7.3

W

wardrobe /'wɔːdrəʊb/ 12.1
washing machine
/'wɒʃɪŋ mə'ʃiːn/ 6.3
(do the) washing up
/'wɒʃɪŋ ʌp/ 9.1
Web page /'web peɪdʒ/ 3.3
wedding /'wedɪŋ/ 9.3
well-paid /wel 'peɪd/ 5.3
wetsuit /'wetsuːt/ 5.2
when /wen/ 2.3
(the) wild /waɪld/ 2.3
wildlife /'waɪldlaɪf/ 4.2
wipe /waɪp/ 6.1
wonderful /'wʌndəfl/ 12.3
wood /wʊd/ 10.1
work (= to function) /wɜːk/ 2.2
worldwide /ˌwɜːldwaɪd/ 1.3
worry about /'wʌri ə'baʊt/ 5.3
(a) wrong number
/rɒŋ 'nʌmbə/ 11.3

Y

You're welcome.
/jɔː 'welkəm/ 9.2

Z

Zoology /zəu'ɒlədʒi/ 6.2
zorbing /'zɔːbɪŋ/ 8.1

Phonetic symbols

Consonants

/p/	pen	/s/	see	/ʒ/	usually
/b/	be	/z/	trousers	/dʒ/	generally
/t/	too	/w/	we		
/d/	do	/l/	listen		
/k/	can	/r/	right		
/g/	good	/j/	you		
/f/	five	/h/	he		
/v/	very	/θ/	thing		
/m/	make	/ð/	this		
/n/	nice	/ʃ/	she		
/ŋ/	sing	/tʃ/	cheese		

Vowels

/æ/	man
/ɑː/	father
/e/	ten
/ɜː/	thirteen
/ə/	mother
/ɪ/	sit
/iː/	see
/ʊ/	book
/uː/	food
/ʌ/	up
/ɒ/	hot
/ɔː/	four

Diphthongs

/eɪ/	great
/aɪ/	fine
/ɔɪ/	boy
/ɪə/	hear
/eə/	chair
/aʊ/	town
/əʊ/	go
/ʊə/	pure

Verb forms

Present simple

Affirmative	Negative	Question
I work	I don't work (I do not work)	Do I work?
You work	You don't work (You do not work)	Do you work?
He/She/It works	He/She/It doesn't work (He/She/It does not work)	Does he/she/it work?
We work	We don't work (We do not work)	Do we work?
You work	You don't work (You do not work)	Do you work?
They work	They don't work (They do not work)	Do they work?

Present continuous

Affirmative	Negative	Question
I'm working (I am working)	I'm not working (I am not working)	Am I working?
You're working (You are working)	You aren't working (You are not working)	Are you working?
He's/She's/It's working (He/She/It is working)	He/She/It isn't working (He/She/It is not working)	Is he/she/it working?
We're working (We are working)	We aren't working (We are not working)	Are we working?
You're working (You are working)	You aren't working (You are not working)	Are you working?
They're working (They are working)	They aren't working (They are not working)	Are they working?

Past simple

Affirmative	Negative	Question
I worked	I didn't work (I did not work)	Did I work?
You worked	You didn't work (You did not work)	Did you work?
He/She/It worked	He/She/It didn't work (He/She/It did not work)	Did he/she/it work?
We worked	We didn't work (We did not work)	Did we work?
You worked	You didn't work (You did not work)	Did you work?
They worked	They didn't work (They did not work)	Did they work?

Past continuous

Affirmative	Negative	Question
I was working	I wasn't working (I was not working)	Was I working?
You were working	You weren't working (You were not working)	Were you working?
He/She/It was working working?	He/She/It wasn't working (He/She/It was not working)	Was he/she/it
We were working	We weren't working (We were not working)	Were we working?
You were working	You weren't working (You were not working)	Were you working?
They were working	They weren't working (They were not working)	Were they working?

Future with *will*

Affirmative	Negative	Question
I'll work (I will work)	I won't work (I will not work)	Will I work?
You'll work (You will work)	You won't work (You will not work)	Will you work?
He'll/She'll/It'll work (He/She/It will work)	He/She/It won't work (He/She/It will not work)	Will he/she/it work?
We'll work (We will work)	We won't work (We will not work)	Will we work?
You'll work (You will work)	You won't work (You will not work)	Will you work?
They'll work (They will work)	They won't work (They will not work)	Will they work?

Present perfect

Affirmative	Negative	Question
I've worked (I have worked)	I haven't worked (I have not worked)	Have I worked?
You've worked (You have worked)	You haven't worked (You have not worked)	Have you worked?
He's/She's/It's worked (He/She/It has worked)	He/She/It hasn't worked (He/She/It has not worked)	Has he/she/it worked?
We've worked (We have worked)	We haven't worked (We have not worked)	Have we worked?
You've worked (You have worked)	You haven't worked (You have not worked)	Have you worked?
They've worked (They have worked)	They haven't worked (They have not worked)	Have they worked?

Irregular verbs

Verb	Past simple	Past participle
be	was/were	been
beat	beat	beaten
become	became	become
begin	began	begun
bite	bit	bitten
break	broke	broken
bring	brought	brought
build	built	built
buy	bought	bought
can/be able to	could	been able to
catch	caught	caught
choose	chose	chosen
come	came	come
cost	cost	cost
cut	cut	cut
do	did	done
drink	drank	drunk
drive	drove	driven
eat	ate	eaten
fall	fell	fallen
feel	felt	felt
fight	fought	fought
find	found	found
fly	flew	flown
forget	forgot	forgotten
get	got	got
give	gave	given
go	went	gone/been
grow	grew	grown
hang	hung	hung
have	had	had
hear	heard	heard
hit	hit	hit
hold	held	held
keep	kept	kept

Verb	Past simple	Past participle
know	knew	known
leave	left	left
lose	lost	lost
make	made	made
meet	met	met
pay	paid	paid
put	put	put
read	read	read
ride	rode	ridden
ring	rang	rung
run	ran	run
say	said	said
see	saw	seen
sell	sold	sold
send	sent	sent
shake	shook	shaken
sing	sang	sung
sink	sank	sunk
sit	sat	sat
sleep	slept	slept
speak	spoke	spoken
spend	spent	spent
stand	stood	stood
steal	stole	stolen
swim	swam	swum
take	took	taken
teach	taught	taught
tell	told	told
think	thought	thought
understand	understood	understood
upset	upset	upset
wake	woke	woken
wear	wore	worn
win	won	won
write	wrote	written

Songs

Unit 1 Jeans on

When I wake up in the mornin' light
I pull on my jeans and I feel all right.
I pull my blue jeans on, I pull my old blue jeans on.
I pull my blue jeans on, I pull my old blue jeans on.

It's the weekend, and I know you're free
So pull on your jeans and come on out with me.
Oh 'cause I need to have you near me, I need to feel you close to me.
I need to have you near me, I need to feel you close to me.

You and me, we'll go motorbike ridin' in the sun
And the wind and the rain.
I got money in my pocket, I got a tiger in my tank
And I'm king of the road again.

I will meet you in the usual place.
You don't need a thing except your pretty face, all right.
I pull my blue jeans on, I pull my old blue jeans on.
I pull my blue jeans on, I pull my old blue jeans on.
Aw, here we go, mama.

You and me, we'll go motorbike ridin' in the sun
And the wind and the rain.
I got money in my pocket, I got a tiger in my tank
And I'm king of the road again.

When I wake up in the mornin' light
I pull on my jeans and I feel all right.
I pull my blue jeans on, I pull my old blue jeans on.
I pull my blue jeans on, I pull my old blue jeans on.

Unit 6 All my loving

Close your eyes and I'll kiss you.
Tomorrow I'll miss you.
Remember I'll always be true.
And then while I'm away
I'll write home every day
And I'll send all my loving to you.

I'll pretend that I'm kissing
The lips I am missing
And hope that my dreams will come true.
And then while I'm away
I'll write home every day
And I'll send all my loving to you.

All my loving I will send to you.
All my loving, darling, I'll be true.

All my loving, all my loving,
All my loving, I will send to you.

Unit 10 Over the rainbow

Somewhere over the rainbow, way up high,
There's a land that I heard of once in a lullaby.
Somewhere over the rainbow, skies are blue,
And the dreams that you dare to dream really do come true.

Someday I'll wish upon a star
And wake up where the clouds are far behind me.
Where troubles melt like lemon drops,
Away above the chimney tops,
That's where you'll find me.

Somewhere over the rainbow, bluebirds fly.
Birds fly over the rainbow, why then oh why can't I?
If happy little bluebirds fly beyond the rainbow,
Why oh why can't I?

Unit 12 This used to be my playground

Chorus
This used to be my playground.
This used to be my childhood dream.
This used to be the place I ran to
Whenever I was in need of a friend.
Why did it have to end? And why do they always say

Don't look back, keep your head held high?
Don't ask them why
Because life is short
And before you know
You're feeling old
And your heart is breaking.
Don't hold on to the past.
Well, that's too much to ask.

Chorus

No regrets? But I wish that you
Were here with me.
Well then, there's hope yet.
I can see your face
In our secret place.
You're not just a memory.
Say goodbye to yesterday.
Those are words I'll never say.

This used to be my playground.
This used to be our pride and joy.
This used to be the place we ran to
That no one in the world could dare destroy.

This used to be our playground.
This used to be our childhood dream.
This used to be the place we ran to.
I wish you were standing here with me.

The best things in life are always free.
Wishing you were here with me.